What Agents Are Saying About
# BEEN THERE, DONE THAT

"Melissa Zavala's wit and wisdom burst from the pages of her latest book, *Been There, Done That: Ten Agent Success Principles from a Short Sale Insider*. Real estate agents, frustrated with the short sale process, will get a chuckle hearing her struggles and successes. Listening to her stories puts our careers into perspective as we identify with her persistence to overcome obstacles using tactical tips and sensible style. Zavala spares no short sale problem as she relates first-hand both the challenges and the joys of serving her clients. Better than "Chicken Soup," this heart-warming book will inspire you to learn success skills, while giving you the humorous perspective so needed to stay sane in the short sale business."

—*Regina P. Brown, Real Estate Broker, Instructor, and Author*

"This book is exactly what real estate agents need to leverage themselves, challenge their perceived limits, and develop the behaviors that lead to remarkable success. New real estate agents can use this book as a guide to building the habits that will propel them to the top of an industry where the 80/20 rule may be more relevant than in any other field of employment. There are myriads of real estate salespersons and so few great Realtors®. The question is *why*? Melissa has successfully cracked the code in this funny, compelling, and very real book about the truth inside this industry."

—*Geri Bekmanis, Realtor®, Keller Williams Realty*

"This book is not just a 'how to' book, but a delightful read full of insights and proven techniques that every real estate agent needs to know. The truths presented along with the humorous stories help us all achieve greater success in this ever-changing crazy world we call real estate. This book should be on every real estate professionals' must read list."

—*Gregg Alexander*, *Broker Associate, Re/Max*

"Through real life anecdotes and years of successful experience closing short sales, Melissa consistently offers valuable coaching for real estate professionals. While most Realtors® and brokers were avoiding the distressed market, and short sales in particular, Melissa embraced this niche market and developed an important professional service for Realtors® and distressed homeowners. Her book offers practical and time-tested principles to help real estate professionals excel in any market!"

—*Mike Gassaway*, *Realtor®, Pacific Pinnacle Real Estate Services*

"As always, Melissa Zavala's insight and expertise shine through in this well-written book for the real estate professional. She brings her wit and humor to what is typically a stressful career and artic-ulates the topics of importance clearly and rationally. She shares the ever-important traits that the excellent real estate professional should attain in this fast-paced profession. Melissa's commitment to better this industry is profound, and I love how she shares it through the real world examples in this book."

—*Kristen Nicholl*, *Senior Loan Officer, Superb Mortgage*

# BEEN THERE, DONE THAT

**ALSO BY MELISSA ZAVALA**

The Essential Daily Planner for Real Estate Agents:
Success in 10 Minutes a Day

# BEEN THERE, DONE THAT
## *Ten Agent Success Principles from a Short Sale Insider*

MELISSA ZAVALA

**MELROSE PUBLICATIONS**
San Diego
2014

www.melrosepublications.com

ISBN 978-0-9860526-2-0
Printed in the United States of America

**To contact the author, visit www.melissazavala.com**
*Book and cover design by Melissa Marquardt*

"Life is a journey, not a destination."

— *Ralph Waldo Emerson*

For my family,
who makes the journey so much fun!

# Contents

# A Note from the Author

When I decided I wanted to write a book about my experience mastering the short sale process, I realized that an ordinary how-to book just wasn't going to cut it.

Not only is the topic of short sales too complex to explain in a simple book, but as the work took shape, I realized that the grueling and sometimes painful process of becoming a short sale specialist had actually become the real adventure.

This book contains several different types of tools for those interested in learning more about short sales, but it focuses primarily on the takeaways I gained while processing and closing thousands of transactions.

These takeaways, like how to apply a laser focus and organized planning to managing multiple complex contracts, are the principles that will remain evergreen, even as the next market trend takes hold, dips, or soars. They are the ones that will last and help you the most in your own real estate career and life.

The crux of this material centers around my list of ten success principles, ones that I believe are at the heart of it all, not only when closing short sale transactions but also when accomplishing pretty much anything you desire.

These principles are the ones I have leveraged in order to succeed.

Focusing on broader personal and professional values rather than just the nitty-gritty step-by-step instructions might seem a roundabout way to go, but it's not. I firmly believe that much of our success is a result of who we are and our character, not just the how-tos we already know.

Never fear, though! I also share plenty of practical real estate information through my very own true, yet sometimes almost too crazy to believe, short sale-inspired anecdotes.

These "Advice from the Front Line" sections will provide valuable context and highlight real-world applications as you develop your expertise, both in short sales and beyond. Be sure to pack your sense of humor for this trip!

To get you up to speed with the unique terminology of short sales, I created a glossary for your use. In the digital version of this book, the first time an industry-specific word is used, there is an active hyperlink to the glossary. The printed version includes this glossary at the back of the book.

In addition to a lively values discussion, you will notice that I mention resources throughout the book to help you delve deeper if you want to do that. I have set up a great webpage that contains lots of valuable information, which will help you to kick-start your short sale adventure.

Go check it out, and enjoy the additional resources that the purchase of this book entitles you to access.

Please enjoy this information, and go do something with it. It will change your life if you let it!

# Introduction

In 2007, a huge life-changing lightbulb went off in my head. It happened so fast, and it was almost like one of those lightbulbs that appear over the heads of cartoon characters to indicate a new and clever idea. It was sudden, obvious, and bright enough for everyone to see.

My husband and I were working as a real estate team at a large franchise. Our business was going well, but it was pretty much like everyone else's real estate business—not much out of the ordinary.

Like a dream come to life, it seemed as if we went to sleep one night with only a few listings but woke up with dozens of **short sale listings.** We had at least twenty-five listings—which meant that we would have almost as many closed transactions—and we were still putting more and more deals into our pipeline!

That's when I recognized the true value and deep potential of the **short sale** transaction.

Short sales, where the seller owes more on the mortgage than the home is worth, began as a largely untapped gold mine in the real estate industry. They were almost all agents' favorite watercooler topic, but not their favorite type of real estate transaction.

## *A Headache No One Wanted*

Nearly every office meeting across the nation had at least one **Realtor**® waxing (not so) poetic on these time-consuming deals. Agents complained about these listings nonstop.

Generally, complaints included inefficient lenders, incompetent employees, and the significant time spent to close a single real estate transaction. Agents did not like how these sales were dominating their time.

Despite all of the complaints, short sale listings have been a great source of income for me. Any smart and business-savvy agent looking for a new niche or a way to make more money would be wise to recognize that sometimes there are hidden opportunities. I noticed this one, and it skyrocketed my success.

## The Lightbulb Didn't Turn On Right Away

In hindsight, my decision to embrace a new niche (something I fondly call my *short sale epiphany*) probably started as a flickering candle a few months before it became that cliché lightbulb moment.

Before realizing the true value of short sales as a way to bring my career to a higher level, the only experience that I had with short sales was listening to the comments made at meetings by other agents at my office.

There was one gentleman at our office who was a jack-of-all-trades. Not only was he a real estate salesperson, but he was also a certified appraiser. In fact, he was even a home inspector. He was a colossal know-it-all. And since I had been schooled from a very young age to respect my elders, I respected and believed everything that came out of his mouth.

"Jack" had a new listing, and it was fairly apparent to his fellow agents that this wasn't a listing that he liked very much.

Jack complained that the listing was sucking up too much of his time. He discussed, in painstaking detail, all of his struggles in communicating effectively with his client's lender. He cursed hour-long hold times and calls rerouted from India to Florida to Arizona.

Jack was managing a short sale and not liking any of it.

## The Problem with Jack

Instead of pitching his property in hopes of putting together a deal with one of the agents at the weekly office meeting, Jack instead aired general frustration. He was irritated by the fact that he could not get his message heard. He felt he had wasted countless hours on unfruitful tasks when he could have been doing other things.

At first, I thought that what he described could not be real. Perhaps it was my naiveté that permitted me to think this way. Did I really live in a world where situations like this existed? I was surprised to hear that lenders could not answer simple questions and that lender communication was so ineffective.

I was also unsettled that Jack was so disparaging in his remarks about the property and the client. But at the same time, I remember asking myself why Jack even bothered to take the listing. After all, aren't all agents trained to only accept listings that they can actually sell?

Even if he could make contact with the bank and they actually agreed to reduce the amount owed, it would take so many long days. I couldn't see a way that this would even be worth all the trouble.

At the end of the meeting, I approached Jack privately in order to elicit more details. He shared more horror stories about inefficiency. I then commented, "When you average out the time spent on this deal, if you even get it closed, you'll probably only make about 57 cents."

It was a bit of a smart-alecky thing to say, perhaps, but I thought he was wasting his time, and I believed that taking that particular listing was not a smart business move.

Looking back at our conversation, I now realize that I put my foot in my mouth big-time. And ironically, the same foot that I put in my mouth on that day in 2007 was the one that has moved me forward to help agents close over 1,500 short sale transactions.

## The Bigger Picture

So what have I really learned? Has this really been just a journey to **closing** lots of short sales?

Not really.

My short sale journey has been one of nearly constant ups and downs, frustrations, steep learning curves, and ultimately, wild success. That journey and how I weathered it, to me, is the meaningful story worth sharing.

I have survived—no, *I have thrived*—in historically adverse market conditions that caused the harsh demise of many of my former real estate colleagues. Even now, as the short sale market ebbs back from its highest crest, years after the initial tidal wave triggered in late 2007, the knowledge I have gained continues to serve me.

I am here to tell you how I did it.

Knowing how to expertly process short sales has had its rewards, but it is the real estate agent I have become by pursuing these difficult, yet enriching transactions that has been the real long-term payoff.

All pride aside, mine is a story of hard-earned victory peppered with challenges and disappointments, resulting in life-affirming professional and personal growth. I grew my business in a market steeped in utter economic chaos, and I am happy to have lived through it.

My foot-in-mouth moment was actually the beginning of an exciting new career. It has been a career that has made me a better agent and a better person.

The communication skills I've gained, the relationship-building tools I can now command easily, and the emotional balance I have learned through the many challenging short sale transactions I've managed are all priceless.

I know you can do the same or better. You too have the opportunity to build your business, regardless of market conditions, using sound, reliable principles that are easy to learn. Well, easy to learn . . . maybe not as easy to master. But you can do that too. I am sure of it!

## Broader Real Estate Lessons

Even though short sales are "dead" and a book about making your career around them is a nonstarter, the point I am here to make is this: my short sale experience taught me a broader lesson. It taught me that it's all about the depth of my skills. Most importantly, it taught me the importance of *soft* skills.

Everyone accepts that the laundry list of hard skills that you need to conquer in becoming an effective real estate professional is long. It includes things like negotiation skills, contract term comprehension, financing knowledge, and more.

You have to be able to research databases, finding the relevant information that your particular transaction needs in order to close.

You have to find leads, develop offers that will be accepted, then coordinate numerous inputs on the way to the final closing.

You have to assimilate tons of information to be able to do your job.

But these hard, analytical skills are not the main ones that can put you a cut above the rest. It's the *soft* skills that can really make a difference—skills like charisma, great communication, empathy, instinct, intuition, and insight.

These soft skills are the ones that develop from practice, commitment, and caring. You have to actually care about your customer, your integrity, and what is best for everyone.

"Win-win" is an overused phrase, but it really applies to the road to success in real estate.

Everyone deserves respect—from the multi-million dollar buyer to the **distressed borrower** trying to sell his one-bedroom condo. And when you actually embrace that philosophy, you will have a winning real estate career.

## *Other Benefits Gained from Working Short Sales*

Aside from the hard and soft skills that were polished by working countless short sale transactions, I realized that there were other benefits I gained from embracing the **distressed property** niche.

### Benefit No. 1: *Maximized market position*

Property values have lowered significantly in many neighborhoods throughout the United States and may not rise to prerecession values for several years. Because of this, it is not uncommon for short sales to be clustered in those specific neighborhoods.

An effective agent with a short sale listing in one of these neighborhoods can market to the other properties within the same neighborhood. It's like short sale listings breed more short sale listings.

Oftentimes, distressed borrowers who are unsure about what to do feel more confident about listing their property as a short sale when one of their neighbors has already taken the plunge.

By fully leveraging this effect, I was able to explode my listings when concentrating on the short sale-affected areas. You can do the same thing in either this niche or any other. Focusing on a logical train of thought and going where that leads will get you the listings that no one else is finding.

### Benefit No. 2: *Elevated status*

Listing, negotiating, and marketing short sales require managing a high level of detail—often much higher than in traditional real estate transactions. You have to pay attention to information on **title reports** and settlement statements in ways not often required in a more balanced market.

It is this relationship with new and different components of the transaction that helps you increase your knowledge. It is this attention to detail that launches your real estate awareness to an entirely new level, one where you are the master of your product. You become the office expert on many things—not just short sales.

By applying myself to intensely focused and detailed work, my overall skills and confidence improved, allowing me to close deals and get leads that I never had the courage to get before. Short sales made me have to focus on those harder things to learn, but learning them was a huge boon. How are you upping your game? Maybe it's time to find a way to challenge yourself.

**Benefit No. 3: *Supercharged real estate career***

If you are a collector of data and you keep up with your sphere, you should be able to leverage your listings and closings into additional significant real estate business over the next several years. That was one of my secrets for wild success within the short sale niche.

To supercharge your real estate career, you need to consistently and methodically seek referrals from sellers and help those sellers and their friends to buy in the future. When you express a genuine interest in helping others, your goodwill can lead to lifelong referrals.

## How to Make It in Short Sales

Someone recently asked me whether I could provide guidance on how to be successful working short sales.

It's not the first time that someone has asked me that question. Over the past several years, I have received countless calls and e-mails asking me for the "secrets" to my success with short sales.

But on this day, the question prompted me to reflect on my journey.

What things do you need to know in order to process short sales? How do you get the lenders to respond? How do you get through the red tape quickly and efficiently?

It was in those thoughts that I came to this conclusion: pretty much everything you need to know to be successful as a real estate professional, and everything you need to know to be successful in nearly every venture of your life, you can learn from working on short sale transactions.

Maybe you have heard the saying "There's nothing *short* about a short sale." And that's true. The short sale transaction involves so many hairpin twists and turns that even the most skilled driver is often faced with challenges throughout the transaction.

Nevertheless, there are several fundamentals that can help to improve your business skills and make you a real estate master, which can be fine-tuned by your work in the short sale transaction.

## *Ten Agent Success Principles*

Nearly any competent businessperson and real estate agent can master the short sale. However, nobody ever becomes a master of anything by closing just one deal. You have to continually put deal after deal into your pipeline.

Employing these ten success principles will practically ensure that you see regular closings—not only in short sales, but in any real estate transaction that comes your way.

### No. 1: Talk Your Talk – The Principle of Communication

From solving a paperwork nightmare to Lady Gaga to your public image online, the stories I can tell about this principle are nearly endless!

I am here to assure you that your communication has impact, more today than ever before. All your words, and the perceived intention behind them, will be scrutinized.

Whether your communication has a positive or a negative impact is almost entirely up to you. This section will give you dozens of tips and tricks to help you *talk your talk* just a little bit better.

### No. 2: Keep It Together – The Principle of Organization

What do Manolos, mole poblano, and cloud-based apps have in common? They all star in your success plan to keep it together.

You're going to meet the Imelda Marcos of Westwood and learn about her amazing shoe collection. You'll discover my ten favorite tools for effective time management, and you'll learn what an ancient Mexican culinary treat has to do with your real estate career.

In order to keep it all together and appear as a well-oiled machine, an agent needs to have excellent organizational skills and a good, solid system or infrastructure. This section will guide you from chaos to order.

## No. 3: Never Give Up – The Principle of Determination

We talk about bank bullies, then ride the roller coaster of intense contract negotiations, and then finish by dispelling some urban myths about Chihuahuas and short sales. We do all of this while learning the ins and outs of the principle of determination.

In this section, you will unleash your superpower of determination and use it for good.

On top of all that, we'll see how to get a refund on defective dishware a full three years after it was purchased. Who said we have to learn about short sales and success principles with only business analogies? Not me!

## No. 4: Learn to Earn – The Principle of Professional Development

See drive time news radio in a whole new light as we move on to the principle of professional development.

We'll do a happy dance when we get a **short sale approval letter**. We'll contemplate the joy of RSS feeds. We'll discuss what to do if someone offers to sell you a bridge (hint: say no) and talk about the hazards of buying a car on Craigslist. All this under the guise of the principle of professional development!

Whether you are a bright-eyed newbie or a seasoned "old-timer," when it comes to real estate, knowledge is power. By applying some powerful step-by-step ideas about how to grow professionally, you'll be well on your way to earning from your learning.

### No. 5: Use Your Head – The Principle of Ingenuity

Whether you had a rich dad or a poor dad, the principle of ingenuity demands that you find a new way of looking at everything.

We'll cover the advantage of thinking inside the **short sale lender's** box and how to avoid real estate suicide. We'll reinvent ourselves by chasing some remarkable purple cows to a new point of view.

While it may seem silly, agents gifted in seeking unconventional solutions often solve difficult problems and, as a result, see increased sales. This section teaches you how to do that.

### No. 6: Respect the Routine – The Principle of Commitment

Are you committed enough to practice for years and years, like Fosbury, when he invented the Fosbury flop? Are you committed enough to apply my Rule of Eleven or practice the twelve habits of top short sale agents until you get them down? Are you committed enough to dominate your niche like a rock star by skillfully marketing to your often-overlooked sphere of influence?

While we debate if cash is still king and whether short sale lenders play favorites, we also cover the deeper lesson within a chocolate chip cookie fiasco.

It's all in the routine, and it's good to respect the routine. Find out how and why here.

### No. 7: Trust in Change – The Principle of Adaptability

Can sliding into sexy skintight spandex and dancing around at the school fair or earning a letterman jacket to win the girl of your dreams grease the wheels of change? It worked for Sandra and Danny, but what about you? Can an old dog learn new tricks?

Whether taste-testing chocolate bacon cupcakes or considering if a woman was the real Shakespeare, being adaptable pays off. Your competitive advantage is your secret weapon against the sands of time. In this section, you will gain lots of tools to help you discover and recognize your ability to go with the flow.

## No. 8: Have a Heart – The Principle of Empathy

Banks are like puppies, and popcorn does not substitute for great customer service. There, I said it. You can be the best paper pusher in the world, but you'd be nowhere if you were not sensitive to the emotional needs of the people you work with.

In this section, I share an anecdote about a slightly sad emotional match that was not made in heaven and the most surprising and best way to get your short sale approved, plus I'll give you tons of tips on how to connect—really connect using empathy and sincerity—with your clients.

## No. 9: Lend an Ear – The Principle of Attention

Auntie Mabel is coming to visit, and she has a single message to deliver—disclose! Add in the tough love I deliver when I say that agents need to shut up, and the ear you lend will be burning.

Times have changed, and you have to pay attention. Pay attention to your clients by deeply listening and to the market by closely observing. You have to ask good questions and be quiet to hear the answers.

In this section, we will discuss why it is so vitally important that you pay attention. Yes, you need to hear this.

## No. 10: Know When to Quit – The Principle of Acceptance

You can lead a horse to water, but you can't make him drink. Sometimes the rules really are the rules. And delivering hard news is a skill you have to conquer. Simple message: get over it, and get on with it.

You have to know what to do to stop a **foreclosure** or when your buyer takes a hike. You have to stay classy and know when you are working a deal that won't close. It's all about lead generation so that the failures don't crater your entire budget. This section gives you the 411 on all of that in spades.

# 1

# TALK YOUR TALK
## The Principle of Communication

Communication is one of the most important skills that we can ever learn. It leads to success or failure in everything that we do—whether we're communicating to meet deadlines and achieve results or communicating with friends, family, and business partners to build stronger relationships.

Sadly, we are not always taught how to communicate properly at school; it's something we pick up from those around us. Unless we are lucky enough to have good communicators in our midst, we can often develop bad habits.

It is simply impossible to become a great real estate agent without being a great communicator. Real estate professionals can be great talkers, but there is a huge difference between talking and communicating.

Strong communication skills in real estate are used when working with buyers, sellers, and our fellow agents. They're also necessary when working with affiliates and associated professionals, including attorneys, settlement officers, **title insurance** representatives, and **mortgage lenders**.

Never have my communication skills proved to be more vital to me than when I began to process and negotiate my own short sale transactions at the beginning of, and throughout, the **Great Recession.**[1] Talking my talk became crucial.

## The Nightmare Begins

In early 2008, I had this totally unbelievable experience with a now-defunct organization called Litton Loan Servicing. I remember the details of the transaction as if it were yesterday. In fact, I even remember the unique lines of the seller's signature on all of the documents in his **short sale package**.

Like all short sales before this one (at that time, I only had around thirty under my belt), I collected and assembled a complete short sale package to send to the lender. In this case, Litton Loan Servicing was that lender.

As was the correct procedure at the time, I telephoned the mortgage lender in order to obtain their fax number so that I could submit a **third-party authorization**. In the same call, I also obtained the fax number for the **Loss Mitigation** Department, where the short sale package was to be submitted.

I had assembled over fifty pages of documents into a neat pile, with a cover sheet, numbered pages, and a loan number on every page—a picture-perfect short sale package. I then faxed the package to the fax number provided to me over the phone.

As was customary, I waited three business days and telephoned the servicer in order to confirm that the short sale package had been received. I was hoping for an easy nonevent because I was ready to discuss the next steps in this particular short sale.

---

[1]*In February 2010, the Associated Press added "Great Recession" to its style guide, with the explanation that "Great Recession," when capitalized, refers specifically to the recession that began in December 2007 and became the longest and deepest since the Great Depression of the 1930s.*

I dialed Litton, input the loan number, and waited on hold for several minutes. I finally heard the voice of a customer service representative in Loss Mitigation come on the line.

The customer service representative went through the whole rigmarole of verifying my identity, the loan number, the property address, the seller's name and contact information, and my name and contact information.

The customer service representative then asked the purpose of my call. I replied, "I'm calling to confirm that you have received the short sale package that I faxed to you three days ago."

The representative responded after looking at her computer screen. She said, "No, we have no record of receiving a fax or a short sale package."

She then suggested that I wait an additional three days and call back—perhaps even try to fax the short sale package again. I took her name and documented our conversation in my communication log.

## Groundhog Day Do-Overs

I refaxed the exact same package to the exact same fax number and waited another three business days. I made the same phone call and completed the same verification ritual. Again . . . no short sale package.

I recorded my conversation with Litton in my communication log and then faxed the package *again*. I went on to make another call to the servicer three days later.

This went on and on. I completed the same ritual nine times in a thirty-day period. The customer service representatives at Litton could never confirm that they received the package.

Each time I sent a fax, I retained the fax confirmation report. These confirmation reports indicated to me that the fax arrived at its destination. Yet each time that I called to confirm receipt, the Loss

Mitigation Department employees told me that they did not have my fax.

They repeatedly verified that I had the correct fax number and correct loan number. Yet still, they had no record of my client's short sale package ever being received.

When the short sale package was not received after the ninth fax, I asked the customer service representative in Loss Mitigation what she suggested that I do. Obviously, the recommended means of submission was not functioning effectively. She stated, "Please fax your package again." She went on to provide the fax number, a number that I had already committed to memory.

"If you have not been able to successfully receive my fax the previous nine times, what makes you think that the tenth time will be successful?" I squawked into the phone. I confess I was starting to get quite frustrated.

"All I can say is that you need to fax your package to Loss Mitigation," she responded.

By then, I was turning bright red. It's possible that steam was actually coming out of my ears and my nostrils. It took all of the self-control that I could muster not to push my arm through that phone line.

Strangling that employee on the other side of the phone line was what I wanted to do at the time. Effective? Maybe not, but probably satisfying.

## Taking Matters into My Own Hands

It was at that moment, when I hung up from that ninth phone call, that I knew that I had to take matters into my own hands.

If Litton Loan Servicing employees could not help me get my message heard or help me get my client's short sale package into the right hands at their own company, I had to take a different tack. I needed to find a way to get this short sale moving on my own.

So with the help of this wonderful thing called the Internet and the excellent research skills that I mastered in graduate school, I got to work.

I compiled a list of all of the top executives and members of the board of directors at Litton Loan Servicing. I crafted a business letter that apologized for going to such great lengths to get my message heard. I then went on to explain that I was facing challenges in having my faxes received by their Loss Mitigation Department.

I sent my letter and package via overnight mail to the executive offices and also converted it to pdf, sending it as an attachment via e-mail to twelve of the top executives at Litton.

In just twenty-four short hours, I received no less than six calls from Litton employees and was told that an executive liaison would be assigned to handle my short sale and any others for which I might need assistance in the future.

## Tips for Effective Business Communication

It was on that day that I realized that writing professional letters, knowing my audience, understanding my topic, and communicating concisely and effectively—skills that I mastered in college—were going to take me far. The four tips included here have greatly maximized the impact of my communication.

### Tip No. 1: *Understand your audience.*

Before you develop any sort of communication, it's a good idea to get to know your target audience. You can communicate until you're blue in the face, but if your message falls on deaf ears, then you are wasting your time.

Real estate professionals who understand their target audience can be more effective in getting their message heard.

### Tip No. 2: *Know what you are talking about.*

Whether you are writing to the chief operating officer at a major lending institution or whether you are contacting another local real estate agent, always be certain that you have a strong command of your subject matter.

If you don't possess subject matter expertise, few people will give you the time of day.

### Tip No. 3: *Be specific and concise.*

It's much better to be specific than ambiguous. Always communicate with clarity. Simple and concise is always better than complicated and confusing. Time has never been a more precious commodity than it is today.

It is critical that real estate professionals learn how to cut to the chase and hit the high points. You don't want people to tune you out before you get to your main point.

### Tip No. 4: *Kill 'em with kindness.*

I know that you have a lot to say. You can bet that I had quite a bit that I wanted to say after so many calls to the Loss Mitigation Department at Litton Loan Servicing. But when you wear your emotions on your sleeve or spit bullets, you may burn bridges to future success.

Be professional in all of your business communications, and never lose your cool—no matter how hot-tempered you might feel.

Not only have these tips for effective communication allowed me to get my message heard, but they have (on countless occasions) permitted me to receive lots of other benefits, including assignments to special liaisons at major lending institutions and cell phone numbers of high-level executives and even one bank president.

It's just amazing what professional communication can do—isn't it?

## ADVICE FROM THE FRONT LINE

### *Disappearing Paperwork Insanity*

When it comes to short sales and working with the lender, communication is not always a two-way street. Unfortunately, lots of times you leave messages, send e-mails, or fax items, and you receive no acknowledgment that anyone is actually working on your file.

Because short sale communication is often one-sided, it is extremely common for a real estate agent to put together a short sale package and fax it off to the bank only to learn three weeks later that the package has not been received.

Why is that?

There are several legitimate reasons why the bank cannot confirm receipt of your package. Understanding these reasons may make your future short sale packages get processed more quickly or actually arrive at their destination.

**Reason No. 1:** *You might've gotten the number wrong.*

It's not uncommon for customer service representatives at banks that receive files via fax to provide incorrect fax numbers. Each lender has different fax numbers for each of their departments. This makes obtaining the correct fax number from the bank employee at the first tier of support a bit challenging.

**Reason No. 2:** *You may not have documented the loan number clearly or correctly.*

There are bank employees whose job it is to receive electronic files and then electronically link those faxes or files to loans. If you have incorrectly typed a loan number, if the loan number is not crystal clear, or if your fax or pdf is blurry, your package may not make it to the right spot.

**Reason No. 3: *People make mistakes.***

When faxing your client's short sale package, you are at the mercy of a bank employee who, like all of us, may be having a bad day or may not be focused on the work at hand. This employee may incorrectly enter a number or not properly associate your package with the right loan.

For these three reasons, it is vital to confirm receipt of the package forty-eight hours after you have faxed it.

Continue to contact the lender every forty-eight hours until you can confirm that the package is received. After all, the best communication with the short sale lender occurs on a two-way street.

## *Don't Get Tripped Up on Jargon*

Sometimes the secret to great communication is hidden in the words you choose. Although some say, "It's not what you say, but how you say it," in short sales, it can easily be as much about what you say as how you say it.

You are probably already aware that the word "friend" now appears in the dictionary as a verb. Thanks to Facebook, people can now *friend* each other. "Friend" not only means what it used to mean, back when it was just a noun, but it has also expanded and changed with the times.

We have to do the same thing with our own communication. Knowing and properly using the relevant short sale jargon and terminology can help in getting your loan processed or your deal pulled together in a timely fashion.

Words matter. A strong working knowledge of the right words to use at the right time can make or break your deal.

For example, a few years back, I had a lunch meeting with the manager of several branches of a real estate franchise, and he said something to me that I still remember. He said, "I love this word '**escalate**.' With short sales, it takes on a whole new meaning." And he was right. It does.

I would bet dollars to donuts that most bank employees who currently use the word "escalate" to address the status of short sale files did not even have this word in their lexicon a few years back.

The word "escalate" refers to taking it up a notch. In the wacky world of short sales, when you *escalate* your issue, you ask that it be addressed by a supervisor, a manager, a vice president, or even the chief executive officer.

There's another word that also takes on a whole new meaning when processing short sales. That's the word "**investor**."

The investor is generally the company or individual who owns the note on a property. For example, a bank employee may state that the investor does not approve closing cost credits or that the investor needs to sign off on the file.

Unlike more traditional real estate transactions, this investor should not be confused with the buyer that purchases a home as an investment.

When the lender says "the investor," here's what it actually means: it means that the representative you are speaking with works for a servicing organization or **mortgage servicer**.

The mortgage servicer has an arrangement with the investor (the owner of the note) to provide mortgage servicing, which includes such activities as collecting mortgage payments and processing your short sale.

There have been times when agents have told me to make sure the bank knows about the termite damage or issues with the roof. These agents want to ensure that the short sale decision takes this information into account.

Of course, it's always a good idea to let the institution know about property defects. You can even provide photos and repair bids.

If the short sale lender is a mortgage servicing organization, however, that very same information is then conveyed from the servicer to the actual investor. And believe it or not, that communication can sometimes get a bit muddled.

**Fannie Mae** and **Freddie Mac** are investors. Major financial institutions throughout the nation service loans for Fannie Mae and Freddie Mac.

In addition to these two big investors, there are also many private investors whose guidelines and decision-making philosophies are more guarded.

As society changes, so does our language. Words such as "escalate" and "investor" have taken on new meaning as a result of changes to the economy and the real estate market.

It's our job to understand these nuances and their implications and work those implications to our advantage.

Understanding the meanings of words within the context of your transaction takes a little time and effort but can make all the difference in getting the sale closed. It helps to pay attention and choose your words carefully.

When you possess knowledge of technical jargon, you demonstrate subject matter expertise. And it is this very expertise that will improve your ability to communicate with all parties in a real estate transaction.

## Communicate Beyond the Seven Percent

One thing is for certain: short sale agents and all Realtors® (even if they are not working in the distressed property market) need to be very careful to use language that does not offend. It's very easy to type out an e-mail and hit the send button without rereading to check for sensitivity.

Oftentimes, when writing e-mails, your thoughts and feelings can be misread or misinterpreted. That's why, despite all of the technology available, it doesn't hurt to actually pick up the phone or, if possible, set an appointment to meet face-to-face.

According to a study conducted in 1967 by Dr. Albert Mehrabian, communication takes on three forms: words, voice quality, and body language. A total of 7 percent of the meaning of the communication comes from words, 38 percent from voice quality, and 55 percent from body language.

Based on these statistics, it seems fairly clear that body language and voice quality are what is going to help you get that next listing or convince that buyer to make an offer on the lovely home you saw just the other day.

Voice quality might also include a phone call with a bank employee that convinces him to get the short sale approval fast.

But you have to wonder whether short sale lenders are aware of Dr. Mehrabian's study.

By making it virtually impossible to have a conversation with a decision maker at a lending institution, and with more and more banks beginning to use **Equator** or other online platforms, it may be more than just efficiency and increased productivity that the short sale lenders are attempting to achieve.

Separating the caller from the decision maker, and discouraging any conversation beyond a message on a computer screen, makes it easier for bank employees to move forward and make a quick decision.

With this more automated process, the listing agent ends up at a real disadvantage, with only a 7 percent chance of getting a more nuanced and considered message across (since the communication is limited to the computer).

To counteract this disadvantage, it becomes even more important to have personal contacts at the lending institutions—people who you can talk to when things are not going quite right. Relying on just the automated process is not the most effective way to go.

Choosing your communication wisely and spending the time to nurture contacts at all the major lending institutions will help you get short sale approvals faster and more easily. You'll also have the added benefit of being able to communicate beyond the 7 percent.

## ADVANCING TO NEW TERRAIN

### Twelve More Tips for Effective Business Communication

The ability to communicate—and communicate well—is one of the biggest components of success in the field of real estate.

You could be an excellent paper pusher, an amazing social media specialist, or even a highly skilled market analyst, but if you're unable to promote your services and communicate effectively with prospects, clients, and colleagues, your sales potential will be limited.

Effective business communication is key to finding potential clients, meeting with clients and prospects, providing customer service, networking professionally, and marketing your business and your services.

Improving your communication skills will pave the way to your increased success—whether you are a newbie or a top-producing agent.

### Find Potential Clients

When you are an independent contractor, you are essentially running your own show. Your livelihood depends upon your ability to sell your services.

Because of this, you need to be able to convince buyer and seller prospects that you are the best person for the job. The communication tips provided here will assist you in meeting that goal.

**Tip No. 1:** *Ask the right questions.*

A vital part of selling your services is being able to understand the customer's needs. You can do this by asking questions in order to understand what the customer may need.

Once you have a clear understanding of what your prospective client needs, you can sell your services as the best possible option, identifying how you will meet those needs.

**Tip No. 2:** *Communicate professionally.*

Your professional communication will help in finding new clients and in negotiating contracts, among other things. Always take time to carefully proofread all letters, e-mails, and marketing materials.

Make sure that the tone and language of your advertising copy send the right message. When on the telephone, answer professionally, and speak clearly and competently at all times.

## Meet with Clients and Prospects

Client meetings, even those that take place over the phone or on Skype, are an integral part of every successful business. Follow these tips to make your meetings as productive as possible.

**Tip No. 3:** *Schedule and prepare thoroughly.*

Everyone is busy, so scheduling your meetings in advance ensures that you and your clients have uninterrupted time to confer. Once your meeting is scheduled, prepare an agenda for your meeting.

Sharing the agenda for the meeting in advance increases efficiency and productivity by giving both you and the client an opportunity to fully prepare.

**Tip No. 4:** *Speak and then listen.*

It's always tempting for a salesperson to speak convincingly to a prospective client. But the truth is that when an individual is oversold, this person is made to feel that his or her input is not important.

Slow down, and remember that communication goes both ways. Establish a rhythm that allows everyone to express his or her thoughts.

### Tip No. 5: *Follow up in writing.*

While you may be taking notes during a meeting, the other party might not be. It's a good idea to always follow up with an e-mail after the meeting, providing an overview of the discussion to make sure that everyone is on the same page.

Summarize what was agreed on, review issues that were raised, and lay out the next steps when applicable.

## Provide Customer Service

Your clients want to feel that they are your top priority. You can make them feel this way by providing a high level of customer service. Try these things to improve your customer service.

### Tip No. 6: *Ask for feedback.*

One way to maintain long-term relationships with your clients is through open lines of communication. Ask for your clients' input on how things are going and how they feel about the service you're providing.

This can be accomplished by inquiring at the end of the transaction, during ongoing conversations, or through formal surveys. You can solicit reviews on Yelp or Trulia, or you can utilize an online service such as SurveyMonkey.

### Tip No. 7: *Address problems.*

If clients are unhappy, don't ignore their complaints. Ask them why they are unhappy and what you can do to make things right. The longer you wait to address a problem, the worse it will get.

Address all problems aggressively, and provide useful solutions. Your willingness to face problems head-on tells the client that you care about their satisfaction.

### Tip No. 8: *Try a different tack.*

If a problem with your client stems from miscommunication, try a different method of communication. If you have been handling everything via e-mail or text message, schedule a phone call to clarify things.

Always carefully consider what kind of information is best delivered in person or over the telephone versus what can appropriately be delivered via e-mail or text message.

## Network Professionally

Networking opportunities, conferences, and other live events can take your business to a new level. The following tips will help you get the most from professional networking activities.

### Tip No. 9: *Communicate confidently.*

Be confident, and use body language to support that confidence. Make eye contact, shake hands, and smile while communicating at live networking events.

Bring business cards to give to everyone you meet, and remember to relax and act naturally—nobody likes feeling as if they're pitched.

### Tip No. 10: *Practice introducing yourself.*

If you are not a social butterfly, it may be challenging to attend networking events. Practice introducing yourself, and be prepared and ready to answer common questions about your business and what you do.

You always want to feel relaxed and comfortable when meeting new people.

## Advertise Your Business or Your Services

Whether you market your business online, in person, or through traditional advertising, communication is key to brand awareness. Here are two ways to increase the impact of your marketing.

**Tip No. 11: *Be responsive.***

A big part of marketing is being available to your target audience and following up when necessary.

If you market your business online—including Twitter, Facebook, and blog posts—watch for and immediately respond to comments, questions, and complaints.

**Tip No. 12: *Write well.***

You can't successfully promote your business if your marketing materials are not clear and concise. Always include a call to action, which tells prospects what you want them to do.

If you are not a writer, consider hiring someone to help you draft copy that attracts prospective clients, generates leads, and calls prospects to action.

## If All Else Fails, Adapt Accordingly

One rarely discussed component of effective communication is the ability to adapt when necessary. Sometimes we need to be prepared with a contingency or backup plan. Of course, if you use the twelve tips I provided, you may not need a contingency plan.

If you feel that your conversation, meeting, or e-mail communication has run amok, you need to be able to change things on the fly.

To mix it up, use great questions, humor, stories, analogies, and relevant data. When needed, add statements, and create conversation that build confidence and trust.

Strengthening your communication skills is worth the time and effort, and you may be pleasantly surprised by how much you will benefit from the time spent polishing your interactions with others.

## *Is All Publicity Good Publicity?*

Great communication, in your real estate career and beyond, is more than just how you conduct yourself on the phone or in **listing appointments**. As previously noted, it applies to your online presence too.

Anytime that I consider the importance of a professional online presence, I recall a news story about music sensation Lady Gaga's behavior at a New York Mets game.

At this particular baseball game, Lady Gaga publicly raised her middle finger to the audience. Because of this inappropriate behavior, Mets security officials moved her to comedian Jerry Seinfeld's empty luxury box.

Upon learning that Lady Gaga was moved to his empty seats, Seinfeld became angry. He felt that this move (made without his permission) was considered a reward or an upgrade, which only served to encourage what he perceived to be negative behavior.

In a way, I think that this particular news story brings to light the importance of maintaining control of your public image, both "onstage" and off. And when considering your own public image, this particular news story does provoke thought.

On the one hand (and to a degree), I see the merits of behaving like Lady Gaga. She is dramatic, and drama creates hype. In Lady Gaga's case, this hype will sell more albums.

At the same time, what message does this behavior ultimately send to children, her family, and those around her about public decency and respect for others?

So where do you stand?

Are you a Lady Gaga or a Jerry Seinfeld? How are you communicating online? How does your public image hold up in the light of day for all to see? Do you believe that all publicity is good publicity?

## *Managing Your Public Image*

Do you realize that people—potential home buyers and home sellers—watch your every move? Are you aware that the way you behave online could have long-term effects on your business? Do you intentionally do and say provocative and controversial things?

Unless you avoid marketing altogether, as a real estate professional, you have a public image.

Keep in mind that your public image is everywhere online. This image may include your Facebook profile page, your Facebook fan page, your Twitter account, your LinkedIn account, your blogs, your videos, and your public comments on the blogs of others.

In your blog posts and comments, do you treat others with respect and decency, or do you comment aggressively in order to create hype and draw attention to yourself and your business?

In responding to others who may disagree with you, do you lash out with vitriol and intolerance? Do you intentionally trigger hot-button issues just to have fun by verbally jousting?

Is your online behavior how you would act if that same person were there in the room with you physically? If not, time for a body check.

Real estate experts who are often in the eye of the public should behave calmly and rationally. It's always best to comment intelligently and politely disagree.

When you do this, you assert yourself as the professional that you want others to hire and do business with in the future. You walk your walk.

Do you believe that any publicity—even bad publicity—is better than no publicity?

It's a tough call. No matter where you stand on the issue, be sure that you make a conscious and deliberate decision about the message you want to send through your online presence.

## *Your Online Presence Communicates You*

Frequently, when I am on social media, I notice real estate professionals communicating inappropriately. It can be a dangerous thing to take a hard stand, especially with controversial topics like politics.

How you are communicating can negatively impact your career. For example, during the 2012 presidential election, one of my colleagues, a local real estate agent, let it all hang out.

What do I mean by that? Well, on her Facebook page, she shared her especially candid thoughts about the election. She went beyond just sharing news. She joined in the fray.

Many people perceive this behavior as a big no-no.

If you have any friends at all on Facebook, then they see your posts. Frequently, your posts can also be viewed by friends of friends, hence the social network experience.

What if an individual who is a prospective client sees that you voted for the incumbent and the prospective client disagrees with that choice? Wouldn't you be alienating a prospective future client with your candor?

I bring up the need for caution in public forums at my office meetings to help agents make more calculated decisions about their public persona. Even the most seemingly innocent subjects can be problematic.

To illustrate my point further, consider the following personal example. I suppose it may, in its own right, cause me to lose a few prospective clients, but let's hope not.

I exercise regularly and am a big fan of hot yoga—yoga in a heated room.

One of the real estate agents who works in my office said that when he hears that I practice yoga, in his mind, he immediately thinks that I chant and meditate. Other people may think that I must be a vegan, a liberal, or perhaps even a communist.

Now here's the rub—this is all because of the fact that I shared information about a hobby.

As a result of sharing that I like to participate in this form of exercise, I have potentially alienated all meat eaters as well as others who have strong feelings about certain aspects of yoga. All of these images are conjured even though I don't chant and I wouldn't turn down a cheeseburger from In-N-Out.

It is important to be cautious and deliberate in the information that you present online because it is out there for all to see and judge.

I admit that there are two sides to this coin; the downside is alienation, and the upside is, as the old adage goes, "all publicity is good publicity."

Frequently, individuals in the public eye say and do things in order to capture our attention through our disagreement, as in the earlier example of Lady Gaga at the ball game.

As a real estate agent, you don't necessarily have to capture attention through disagreement or negative behavior. If you decide to, realize the risk you are taking, and stay aware of the response you are getting. If it's what you prefer, great. If not, make an adjustment.

Generally speaking, you'll have to decide for yourself the risk versus the return. When considering professional communication, both online and off, keep in mind that the fray is not always where everyone wants to be.

---

Sample letters for use when corresponding with short sale lenders as well as short sale package preparation information can be found on the *Been There, Done That* resource page at www.melissazavala.com

# 2

# KEEP IT TOGETHER
## The Principle of Organization

One of the skills required of a good short sale listing agent, **short sale negotiator**, and real estate agent in general is the ability to keep everything well organized.

Busy real estate agents have many deals going at one time, serving a mix of both buyers and sellers.

These successful agents are managing their websites, their paid advertising, and their social media accounts. They are negotiating and prospecting and more, all while keeping current buyers and sellers happy by providing excellent customer service.

In order to keep it all together and appear as a well-oiled machine, an agent needs to have excellent organizational skills and a good, solid system or infrastructure.

### The Imelda Marcos of Westwood

The most well-organized person that I've ever known was my very own grandmother.

As the story goes, she was so well organized and efficient with her time that she would set the table for breakfast the following morning before she went to bed every night.

But my recollection of her organizational skills is slightly different.

As a young girl, I loved to go visit my grandmother at her Westwood apartment. In my eyes, she was the Imelda Marcos of Westwood with shoes galore, and what small girl doesn't like to play dress-up?

The master bedroom of her apartment had a very long hallway, flanked by mirrored sliding closet doors. When you slid open the door on her side of the closet, you would see that the bottom three feet of the entire closet were stacked with boxes and boxes of women's shoes.

While you may not be surprised to hear of a woman with lots of shoes, what was unique about this shoe collection is that each and every shoebox was covered with patterned cream-colored contact paper. In addition, each box had a label on it with a description of the shoes inside.

All boxes were categorized by color and style according to the information noted on the label. In this way, she could easily find the shoes she required for each specific occasion.

What young child would not love to pretend they were working in a shoe store when in a closet designed and organized in this manner?

## Three Lessons Learned from Grandma's Closet

While many folks may consider this system of organization excessive, I loved it. It made for an awesome game of shoe store.

Even though Grandma's actions may sound strange now, many decades later, she was actually very clever. There are many admirable qualities that arise out of setting up a system for whatever aspect of your life may require it—whether it is the administration of your home or the management of your real estate business.

### Lesson No. 1: Good infrastructure takes time to set up.

There is no question that it took Grandma lots and lots of time to cover each and every box with contact paper and then prepare the labels.

Can you imagine the time saved on the back end when it would only take her a second or two to locate the shoes she desired?

Developing a strong organizational system cannot be rushed; however, in the long run, there will be a significant time savings.

### Lesson No. 2: *Benefitting from your system requires discipline.*

If you want to get the most out of what you do, you need to create your own processes and stick to them.

It doesn't matter whether it's the contact paper and labels or saving your files in a specific document management system; if you deviate from your organizational plan, you'll pay.

Just imagine what would have happened if Grandma did not put her shoeboxes back in the same order. How long would it take her to find what she was looking for? Would her system still have merit? Would yours?

### Lesson No. 3: *The devil is in the details.*

This common adage about details rings true. It means that whatever a person does needs to be done completely and thoroughly.

If not completed in a detailed manner, the same plans and procedures that can lead to success may instead lead to failure. Just because you set up a system like Grandma's doesn't mean that you are going to get the most out of it.

You need to always have contact paper and a label maker, and you must be willing to put those boxes back in the correct order each and every day.

The same goes for the systems in your business.

How do you make notes for your short sale files? Where do you save your documents? Do you have a system for file naming that is consistent and makes things easy to find?

While it is important to maintain well-organized and well-developed systems, it is equally important to recognize that you might not be the one to develop them.

Not all real estate professionals are as well organized as Grandma. Developing strong, solid systems that lead to success often requires more than these three lessons; it may also require hiring an experienced and qualified helping hand.

## ADVICE FROM THE FRONT LINE

### *Prepare for Your Listing Appointments*

Short sale listing appointments can be overwhelming—not only for the prospective client, but also for the listing agent. There is so much to discuss and so much documentation to sign and collect.

In order to make the short sale listing appointment as organized and efficient as possible, here are some tips to help keep you on track.

**Tip No. 1:** *Do your pre-appointment homework.*
It's a good idea to spell out for clients what you will need to collect at the appointment—the items necessary for the short sale package (mortgage statements, pay stubs, tax returns, and bank statements).

Have your to-do list ready in advance, and share it with your sellers before you show up. This gives them the chance to get organized as well, making the entire experience more efficient for everyone.

**Tip No. 2:** *Bring everything you need to the appointment.*
Bring the following items with you to the listing appointment: third-party authorization, **financial statement**, **Form 4506-T**, and blank sheets of paper (for writing the **hardship letter**).

After the sellers sign the **listing agreement**, collect the documents required for the short sale package. Next, have the seller write the hardship letter while you are double-checking that you have collected all of the required paperwork.

When you handle the listing appointment in this way, you will have a complete package with you when you leave.

I've always considered the listing appointment as a predictive window into the efficiency of the transaction. If the short sale seller has all the documentation ready, then I know that the seller is an organized person who is eager and motivated to sell the property in a short sale.

If the short sale seller hems and haws about providing the documentation and blames the bank for this or that, I know that I will have work to do in explaining to the seller how important it is to react quickly when the short sale lender has an immediate request.

Common questions that short sale sellers may ask include those about **mortgage debt relief**, **deficiency judgments**, **HAFA**, and other short sale **incentive programs**. Be sure that you have a strong command of all these topics before setting the appointment.

## Ancient Mexican Recipe for Success

Another aspect of being organized is knowing (and executing) the right steps in the right order at the right time, just as we discussed with respect to the short sale listing appointment.

It may sound funny, but a short sale closing and just about any other real estate transaction is a bit like a recipe for mole poblano.

Have you ever heard of mole poblano? It's a traditional Mexican sauce made famous in the colonial days of Mexico that has over twenty different ingredients and a complex cooking sequence. Chocolate features prominently in mole poblano and gives the sauce its distinct character.

Just like the twenty-plus ingredients in this delicious and spicy sauce, there are at least as many different details that need to be balanced in order to assure that your real estate transaction closes quickly and efficiently.

This type of balance requires you to manage lots of inputs while you push and pull whatever details need to be handled along the way.

I really can't say it enough: organization is your friend, whether dealing with short sales, juggling your household expenses and activities, or solving business-related issues with challenging people.

Know the who, what, when, where, and how of a situation, and you will be golden.

Just as the ingredients of mole poblano need to be added in a specific order in order to assure a certain flavor, so too is it in real estate.

There are key ingredients that, when handled in a specific order, will improve your likelihood of short sale success.

### Step No. 1: *Engage homeowners early.*

Find out whether the homeowner owes more on the home than it's worth. Discuss short sale opportunities in the initial conversations with the homeowner.

Using a chart that shows the differences between a short sale and a foreclosure, explain the benefits of a short sale and how it can help borrowers to avoid foreclosure.

### Step No. 2: *Contact the lienholders before the home is listed.*

Learn whether the homeowner can be evaluated for any of the available special short sale programs, perhaps through the U.S. Treasury.

Find out if the homeowner will qualify for any of the other unique incentive programs offered by specific lenders.

### Step No. 3: *Complete required tasks on time.*

Provide all the necessary documents as quickly as possible in order to keep the process moving along. Communicate with all parties in order to keep unnecessary delays to a minimum.

When provided with a deadline by your client's lender, do your best to meet that deadline.

While there are certainly many more ingredients to a successful real estate closing, these are just a few. It's important to stay organized to cook up a solution for your success.

When working with new clients, always master the recipe for success before moving forward.

## Stay Organized, but Go with the Flow

Real estate professionals always laugh about the grand irony of short sales.

That is, we wait and wait and wait for the short sale negotiator at the bank to finally get to the file. Then all of a sudden, the lender wants something.

They cannot find the listing contract. They do not like a signature. They want updated bank statements. Whatever it is, they want it, and they want it now!

It does not matter that it took eight weeks for your file to finally hit the processor's desk. Now that it is there, it must be dealt with immediately or closed out.

Why is it like this? Well, the reason is quite simple.

To most bank employees, your client is just a file—one more thing on the desk. The faster it is addressed, the sooner they get to move on.

So if you do not respond to a bank request as soon as humanly possible, it's very likely that the bank employee will close or decline your client's short sale file.

As you probably already know, once a bank employee closes out a file (even by error), you may have to start the short sale process all over again from the very beginning.

As if that wasn't bad enough, there's another major drawback of the file being closed out.

If there is or was a postponed **trustee's sale** or foreclosure **auction** date, now the sale may be scheduled again.

Oftentimes, foreclosure auctions are postponed because the bank is working to obtain short sale approval. However, from the short sale lender's perspective, if there is no short sale in process, there is no need to postpone the foreclosure auction.

When things like this happen, you need to go with the flow and work within the system instead of against it. You need to cooperate with the lender and get things done efficiently if you want to receive short sale approval.

In short sales, you have to stay organized, stay on top of your dates, be prepared with documents when they are needed, and be ready for action at a drop of a hat—even if the bank has been dragging behind.

## *Know Your Lender, Know Your Paperwork*

Timing is only one aspect of staying organized. You also have to keep the various lender requirements straight as you work your systems.

When you process or negotiate enough short sales, you become familiar with how each specific lending institution operates.

For example, you will know which banks are unlikely to postpone a foreclosure auction, and you will also know which banks are slow to process your short sale transaction.

When you get an approval from a short sale lender, be sure to look at all of the pages you receive very carefully.

Agents are often so excited about their victory that they tend to overlook the other pages that come with the approval letter. These other pages are the ones that outline, in very specific terms, what has to happen for your deal to close.

Take time to review all of the items and instructions.

Each short sale lender requires a different process at closing—some require that the settlement statement be submitted prior to closing, others want the funds wired in twenty-four hours, and some need all the pages of their documents signed and notarized.

Keeping on top of these different requirements and varying documents and guidelines can be extremely challenging. So it's a good idea to develop a system for handling these items in an organized way.

Real estate professionals may always be multitasking and managing multiple inputs, and often, agents are easygoing as a result.

Banks aren't always that happy-go-lucky. They often return funds if things are not done to their satisfaction. And just imagine how unpleasant a situation will be if the buyer is residing in a home that still has some outstanding financial issues.

## ADVANCING TO NEW TERRAIN

### *One Bad Apple Spoils the Bunch*

Perhaps the worst part of the short sale process is how the inefficiency of the short sale lenders can make even the best and most efficient agent appear to be subpar.

Have you ever heard the saying "Lack of planning on your part does not constitute an emergency on my part"? Well, it's that philosophy that appears to have been adopted by most of the major lending institutions.

Despite the fact that the agent has provided all of the required short sale documentation in a timely manner, all parties need to wait.

They often need to wait while the employee at the bank takes a vacation, goes on medical leave, or just decides he or she is ready to work on your file. It could drive you crazy if you let it.

Even the stories that you relate to your clients about your experience sound like you made them up.

You provide documents and follow up. The employees state that they have submitted documentation for approval and it should be no more than ten days. You tell the client what you know.

Ten days pass, and you have nothing. You call the bank and get a completely different story from the representative that answers the phone.

You then have to call the clients and tell them that the lender actually didn't do what they said. However, you assure the seller (as you have been assured) that we are now on the right path. It will only be ten more days (at least that's what you are told).

Again, the time elapses and no short sale approval. No support from the lender. Nobody returns your phone calls. It is situations like this one that do not bode well for the short sale listing agent. The story of inefficiency is so farcical that it must surely be a lie.

What causes this inefficiency? Is it apathy? Is it lack of training? Is it the fact that the employee feels so comfortable in his or her position that he is not worried about losing his job?

Or perhaps it is the fact that if a bank employee demonstrates extreme efficiency, he might be rewarded with more work instead of dollars.

Whatever the case, stay organized. It's important to log all communication with the lender so that—when push comes to shove—despite the unbelievable stories, it is not you that is going to be out of a job.

## The Stuff Beyond Your Control

Controlling a real estate transaction can be tough. That's because the transaction involves more than just you. And no matter how efficient and organized you might be, stuff will happen that is beyond your control.

You need to simply learn to cope with the fact that things may be out of your control. It will make you a better person to grow this way, I promise.

Although it won't always feel fair, you could easily be held responsible for other parties' inefficiency and lack of organization.

This makes it all the more important that you have your act together so that you can counteract the foibles of all the other so-called professionals involved in the real estate transaction.

Such is life.

As **short sale negotiators** or **real estate listing** agents, we are the middlemen (or middlewomen). We take the short sale package and all of the information provided to us by the short sale seller, and we submit it in a pretty little package to the short sale lender for the lender's review and processing.

We then call or e-mail (or both) a few times a week. We ask the **short sale lender** if they have everything they need in order to process the short sale.

Sometimes they answer, and sometimes they don't. We leave messages. We ask thought-provoking questions. We push, and we prod.

We e-mail the escalation department, the executive offices, and just about anyone that we can find that will push that short sale through the pipeline. But it takes such a darn long time.

That's right. There is absolutely nothing short about a short sale—except for the patience of many of the parties to the transaction. You have to simply keep showing up and doing the work in an organized and efficient manner.

But even if you are not working short sales, there is always the opportunity for a bad apple to spoil the barrel.

Sometimes a client will have loan approval, and then some issue may arise during the underwriting process that could halt or delay the closing. Other times, there could be an outstanding title issue or an unpaid seller **lien** (such as a tax lien or abstract of judgment) that could hold up the closing.

When it comes to situations like these, they are often out of the real estate professional's control, yet many people will lay blame wherever they can. And unfortunately, if your client has a sour experience, it may come back to you—even if the blame lies elsewhere.

It is your level of commitment and dedication to detail where real character comes in.

Situations of sour grapes and how you deal with them are what separate the *wannabes* from the ones who get it done. Choose to be one of the ones who get it done; do that by being efficient and on top of your game.

## How to Make Order from Chaos

A day in the life of a real estate professional can be pretty chaotic. You wake up one day fully poised to smile, dial, and make a pile only to arrive at your office and have to run and unlock a property door or reschedule a home inspection.

Because of the consumer-based nature of real estate, it is often difficult to stay organized and in control of your daily activities.

In order to take control of those daily activities and the destiny of your real estate career, time management should always be your top priority. To make money in real estate, you must make efficient use of your time. You cannot be lazy or procrastinate, and sometimes you won't even get a day off when you want it.

Unfortunately, if you cannot stay organized and follow a strict daily schedule, your success in meeting your goals may be hampered significantly.

Successful agents design plans for achieving their goals. They set short-term and long-term goals, both of which can be achieved with the completion of daily activities.

Since completing daily activities is so important, procrastination is a real estate professional's archenemy. You must always focus on staying motivated and organized. Remember that your income is a direct result of your efforts and achievements.

## Create a Schedule, and Stick to It

Organize your daily tasks, and resign yourself to complete all of them each and every day. Remember that it is important to be realistic and not put too many items on your daily schedule because pushing too hard can be counterproductive.

However, no matter what happens, you must commit to completing all of the items on your to-do list before you rest your head at night.

Schedule the tasks that you hate to do first thing in the morning so that you can get them out of the way. If you despise returning phone calls, get them out of the way as early as possible.

When you complete activities that you don't like first thing in the morning, you feel a great sense of accomplishment, and it is easier to move on to other items on the list.

## Invest Extra Time When Necessary

Whenever you complete all of your work earlier than expected, take advantage of the extra time to bring your business to the next level.

Spend an extra ten minutes doing a bit of what your school-teachers may have called extra credit. Consider one of the following ideas:

- Call a past client.
- Post to social media sites.
- Organize your desk or your e-mail inbox.
- Clean your workspace.
- Read articles on professional development, or watch online webinars.
- Check out the latest real estate news.
- Download new apps and tools that increase productivity.

Believe it or not, doing just one small extra task will have benefits. Even cleaning your desk or sorting through piles of paperwork can be very productive since you will create a cleaner environment for future activities.

## Quit Wasting Time

Sometimes real estate agents get behind on work because they let themselves become discouraged or disappointed. They lament things that don't work out. When you are constantly cycling back to yesterday's activity or problem, you are not moving forward but instead taking a step back.

If a buyer or seller changes his or her mind, remember that it's not the end of the world. If you let yourself become discouraged and you wallow in what could've or should've been, you will only fall further behind.

## Use Technology Effectively

New technology to increase the efficiency of the real estate professional comes out each and every day. You can download software onto your computer, install apps on your smartphone or tablet, invest in a new laptop, and so forth.

When you take advantage of such tools and resources, you can save a lot of time as you will be able to automate many processes.

With the time you save, you'll be able to focus on clients' needs, and your good service will result in more sales.

Top agents are successful because they do an excellent job managing their time. Time management can be achieved by taking advantage of available tools and resources. You need to stay organized and work toward achieving both short-term and long-term goals.

You too can meet your goals through good time management, lack of procrastination, a positive attitude, and the ability to embrace new technologies and tools that may come our way.

## Ten Best Tools for Real Estate Success

In order to be an organized master of your trade, you need to have all of the correct supplies in your tool kit. What would a carpenter do without a hammer and nails? What would a painter do without a brush?

This list includes the best organizational tools, ones I use every day. Using these items effectively will allow for so much increased efficiency that you won't know what to do with all the extra time!

### Tool No. 1: *File folders with separators*

Many agents receive these folders for free from local **escrow** and **title companies**. They are thick legal-size folders with separators and brackets at the top.

Even if you process your real estate transaction virtually, you may want to keep the hard copies of your paperwork organized. These heavy-duty file folders are strong enough to handle even the largest and most challenging file.

### Tool No. 2: *High-speed scanners*

Whoever invented these portable high-speed scanners is brilliant. Depending upon which model you purchase, you may even be able to carry your scanner with you to your listing appointments.

Can you imagine how much time you will save when you scan your clients' documentation and return the originals immediately? Couple that scanner with a pdf-to-fax program (such as eFax or TrustFax), and your days standing next to a fax machine and hoping that it won't jam are a thing of the past.

### Tool No. 3: *High-speed fax machines*

If you are not scanning your documents and then sending them from your computer, you will need a superpowered fax machine with a large document feeder in order to send those eighty-five-page faxes to the short sale lenders.

### Tool No. 4: *Cloud-based storage solutions*

A cloud-based storage system is like a virtual file cabinet in the sky.

In addition to the pleasures of having access to all of your clients' documents wherever you are, you save time and money when your tech-savvy clients upload their documents into a cloud-based storage system—instead of you having to drive to the property to collect them.

### Tool No. 5: *Note apps*

Note apps (such as Evernote) that save pdfs, notes, and even photos are a good way to organize your information.

Since note apps are principally cloud-based, you can access your information anywhere from any location. You can even create customized tags that include such information as the property address or your client's name. With your own easy-to-remember tags, you'll have access to everything in a flash!

### Tool No. 6: *Google Drive*

Google Drive is another great cloud-based system where you can store and create documents related to your real estate transaction. You can even create spreadsheets to record your communication with short sale lenders and the other parties involved in your sale.

Since Google Drive is also cloud-based, you have access to your documents when you need them—even if you are at lunch or heading to a meeting.

### Tool No. 7: *Tablets and smartphones*

Tablets and smartphones are very popular. Since they are small enough to fit in your bag and robust enough to take care of all of your real estate activities, they significantly increase efficiency.

### Tool No. 8: *Calendar apps*

You will want to find a calendar app that syncs across all of your devices. That way, when you set up an appointment or note a task on your computer, you can be reminded of it on your smartphone.

Not only do calendar apps help you save time, but they also assure that you never miss an appointment.

### Tool No. 9: *Electronic signature platforms*

**Electronic signatures** are all the rage. Instead of uploading a pdf and then sending your client a document that needs to be printed and instead of driving to your client's home with a pile of papers that need dates and initials, you can upload everything into the electronic signature platform, and your client can sign all the documents online.

Electronic signature platforms are available for tablets, smartphones, and computers. They save time and money.

### Tool No. 10: *Real estate apps*

There are loads of apps available that can help you do your job more quickly and efficiently. **MLS** apps, seller net sheet apps, mortgage calculators, and others make it easy for you to provide all of the services you need in one simple location—even if it is at the coffee shop or on the side of the road.

It's always a good idea to get your tools organized so that you can provide the best and most efficient service possible. These ten productivity tools will help you to embrace the future of real estate and continue to be successful in your day-to-day activities at the same time.

You can access additional information about how to prepare for traditional and short sale listings on the *Been There, Done That* resource page at www.melissazavala.com

# NEVER GIVE UP
## The Principle of Determination

There are many skills that real estate agents need in order to be successful: marketing skills, technology skills, presentation skills, negotiating skills, and objection-handling skills, among other things.

But the truth of the matter is that the collective value of all of these skills does not compare to the importance of one particular character trait: persistence.

Persistence is one trait that can make up for our deficiencies in other areas. It may allow us to succeed even when there are obstacles in front of us.

Benjamin Franklin said, "Energy and persistence conquer all things." It truly is a unique talent to be able to move forward when everything around you is collapsing. The ability to meet a challenge head-on and breeze past the competition can help agents to overcome many hurdles.

As real estate professionals, most of us know what we need to do, yet sometimes we don't do it. Often, we spend much of our time looking for the one thing that will change our life instead of taking the path of persistence in order to succeed.

Persistence is the one character trait that guarantees success in both your personal and professional life.

## *Persist, and You Will Often Get Your Way*

Several years ago, my husband and I received a very generous gift, something that we very much needed. It was a gift card for a high-end catalog store, and we used the card to purchase a new set of microwave-safe dinnerware. We had the dinnerware for quite some time and used it day in and day out.

Then one day, about two years after the purchase, one of my friends heated up some hot water using a mug from the dinnerware set. She commented to me that the mug was extremely hot to the touch when she removed it from the microwave oven. So hot, in fact, that she had to use an oven mitt to remove it.

After noticing the same phenomenon myself on several occasions, I decided that it was necessary to return the dinnerware. After all, the bottom of each and every piece stated "microwave safe," yet all of the pieces were now hot to the point of burning—and did not appear to be safe for use in the microwave oven.

So a few weeks later, I called the toll-free customer service number for the catalog company. I waited patiently on hold for customer service.

When my call was finally answered, I explained to the customer service representative that I had used a gift card to purchase dinnerware sometime ago. I no longer had the receipt but felt that I needed to return the dinnerware since it was dangerous to use and not microwave safe as advertised.

The customer service representative was friendly and polite and was able to locate the original order by name and mailing address. She informed me that I had owned the dinnerware for nearly three years.

"Unfortunately, ma'am, our company policy states that our items are only warrantied for one year. So there is nothing we can do," she responded.

I don't remember how the conversation had ended, but I knew

that I felt that some major injustice had just befallen me. Not only would they not take back their items that I believed to be defective, but I now had no usable dinnerware and would have to go out a purchase a new set that wouldn't burn anyone when put into the microwave.

I hung up the phone and pondered my next move.

You see, I am always open to hearing both sides of an argument. But if I feel, after hearing both sides, that I still hold the winning argument, my persistence and tenacity take over. I do not give up until my concerns have been addressed accordingly.

Using that philosophy, which underscores my general modus operandi, I decided to research the location of the catalog company's executive offices. Upon securing that information, I drafted a clear and concise e-mail explaining my situation and hit the send button.

Within twenty-four hours, I received a phone call. This phone call was followed up with an e-mail that included a printable UPS label. I was told to package up my merchandise and contact UPS; they would come to pick it up at my door free of charge.

Two weeks later, I received full reimbursement for the dinnerware.

## Three Situations When You Must Persist

It often takes a level of persistence and tenacity—a level that far exceeds what I demonstrated in the return of my dinnerware—in order to get a contract accepted or a short sale approved.

Off the top of my head, I cannot think of a single situation in real estate where it does not pay to be tenacious and persistent. However, here are three situations where it is vital to demonstrate these traits:

### Situation No. 1: *When it's a seller's market*

If you have ever represented buyers in a **seller's market**, then you know that this is no easy feat. When the absorption rate is under one month and each home receives upwards of twenty offers, you cannot throw in the towel. You must persist!

If you consider yourself a real estate agent by trade, you need to be tenacious in order to get your deals to the closing table. Just because your first seven offers were not accepted doesn't mean that you should go out and shop for a new career.

### Situation No. 2: *When you get no response from an advertising campaign*

How many times have you sent out a Just Listed or Just Sold postcard and received not a single communication in return? This doesn't necessarily mean that you should give up.

You might want to consider modifying what you do—perhaps the text or the style of your marketing piece. Or maybe you need to modernize or alter your methods in order to get a better return on your investment. However, none of this means that you need to give up.

### Situation No. 3: *When the lender cannot locate your information*

If you've done more than a few short sales, then you have probably experienced a situation where you've been told that some item that you have faxed, e-mailed, or uploaded has not been received—despite that fact that you have proof to the contrary. It's a common enough problem that it bears repeating here.

If the short sale lender tells you they have not received your fax (and you know that they must have it there someplace), do not give up. Consider alternative methods to get your message heard and receive the answer that you want, just as I did with Litton Loan Servicing.

Tenacity and persistence will make you a rock-solid agent. Not only will these traits help you to successfully accomplish certain tough daily tasks, but these traits will also help you to gain the trust and respect of your clients. It's the right combination of patience, persistence, and politeness that will get you the business you deserve.

---

## ADVICE FROM THE FRONT LINE

### *No Bullies Allowed*

When working with the short sale lenders, each person has his or her role. We are the agents that approach the lender on behalf of the seller in order to make a request for **debt settlement**. However, we often have to contend with an interesting cast of characters in order to get the short sale approved.

When you contact the bank to discuss your short sale, you need to be in a particular mind-set: knowledgeable, experienced, quick on your feet, inquisitive, polite, and professional all at the same time.

When the real price and terms negotiations occur, you must always remember your role. Sometimes the lender will request an increase in purchase price, which you may believe to be unreasonable.

Here are three pointers that will help you get the upper hand when working with the short sale lender and negotiating the purchase price:

**Pointer No. 1:** *Understand the lender's financial investment in the property.*

When the property reverts to the bank, it becomes a nonperforming asset. When the lender holds a nonperforming asset, the lender is also required to hold liquid assets (collateral) at up to five times the value of the nonperforming asset.

Since banks make their money by investing (not by holding liquid assets), it is in the best interest of the lender to get a nonperforming asset off the books as fast as possible.

**Pointer No. 2:** *Remember that banks are not property management companies.*

When lending on the property, the mortgage company did not plan to pay the **homeowner's association** (HOA) dues, utilities, repairs, property taxes, and county tax assessments, among other fees.

If a bank takes the property back in foreclosure, the bank will then be responsible for paying all of the property expenses.

**Pointer No. 3:** *Know that each day, lender losses increase.*

Each and every day that there are no mortgage payments made on a property, the lender is losing money.

Between that, the inability to borrow, and issues arising from deferred maintenance, there are lots of costs associated with a short sale that sits unapproved.

If you are being bullied or strong-armed by a bank employee who says that the bank must net a few more dollars, that bank employee may not understand the "big picture."

The big picture here is that taking this particular asset back into the bank's portfolio will cost the lender hundreds of thousands of dollars in lost borrowing power as well as many additional dollars for all of the property-management related expenses.

Does the short sale negotiator still insist that you raise the purchase price? Perhaps it's time to escalate your file and attempt to speak with someone who understands the value that your short sale brings to the table.

## Overcoming Short Sale Obstacles

If you have ever received a short sale approval letter, you, no doubt, have had a feeling of jubilation like almost no other. It's a huge thrill of victory.

The trials and tribulations of negotiating a short sale, keeping the buyer and seller content, and finessing all of the details make the receipt of the approval letter feel like a multimillion-dollar win on the penny slots in Las Vegas.

Unfortunately, the receipt of the approval letter doesn't always guarantee that the transaction is home free.

There is still a traditional purchase period—complete with an appraisal, an inspection, and even perhaps the obtaining of a loan. Sadly, the transaction could still fall through, even after short sale approval has been obtained.

There are many last-minute hurdles to closing a short sale. Two such hurdles involve property appraisals and liens.

### Hurdle No. 1: *Property appraisals*

Sometimes after the short sale approval letter is obtained, the buyer learns that the lender's appraisal is for an amount lower than the purchase price.

If this happens to you, don't give up hope. Submit a copy of the complete appraisal to the short sale lender for review. Oftentimes, a revised approval at the appraised value is just around the corner.

### Hurdle No. 2: *New liens*

New liens against the property or the borrower often appear during the transaction period. HOA liens are commonplace in the state of California, for example.

If a new lien appears and needs to be satisfied in full before closing, ask the short sale lender to contribute toward the payoff of the lien. You can also ask other parties to the transaction if they would be willing to help satisfy the lien.

The bottom line is, as you've heard before, "it *ain't* over 'til it's over." Even when there are new obstacles to overcome, with a little bit of tenacity and stick-to-itiveness, an approved short sale can result in successful closing.

## Negotiations Are Like a Ride on a Roller Coaster

Sometimes when you are working on a particularly tedious transaction, you feel as if you must be on some sort of wild roller-coaster ride at the amusement park.

While this story may be a bit technical, I share it because it illustrates perfectly the role of tenacity and gives you a closer look into how completely bizarre and unbelievable a single short sale transaction can be.

Several years ago, one of my associates took a short sale listing in the month of January. It was a gorgeous home in a very desirable neighborhood. He received many, many offers on this property.

We contacted the lender, submitted the package, then followed up, followed up, and followed up.

Between January and May of that year, the file was assigned to five different negotiators and canceled or declined a few times for no apparent reason. While reassignment is common, this was excessive. So we contacted the bank's executive offices to see what could be done.

Finally, in late spring, our file was assigned to a special negotiator from the bank's executive offices. She was a sweet, professional woman who really knew how to do her job right.

After almost six months and many negotiators, we ultimately learned that the second lienholder would require $25,000. Unfortunately, we couldn't get past this hurdle.

### Loan Modification . . . WTF!

Our feisty friend at the bank discussed our situation with supervisors and supervisors of supervisors. All agreed that there was nothing they could do except to recommend that the seller apply for a **loan modification.**

Months elapsed while we attempted to help process the loan modification. The seller was dissatisfied with the terms and asked that we discuss further options with the lender. In doing so, the lender responded, "How about a short sale?"

"Really?" I said in my head. "First, you tell me that I cannot do a short sale and that I must do a loan modification. Now you tell me to try a short sale again." I was wondering whether this was some sort of joke.

Thirteen months after the listing was taken, we finally received short sale approval. The second lienholder agreed to accept a more reasonable amount than $25,000, and we were able to get the job done.

Loan modification? Short sale? WTF! (Wow, that's fantastic!)

Tenacity, patience, and the fact that we didn't give up are what got this short sale approved. It doesn't always work out quite this way, but in this case, the long and tedious ride on the roller coaster certainly paid off.

## ADVANCING TO NEW TERRAIN

### *Is Tenacity a Superpower?*

Don't mess with me; I negotiate short sales.

What I've learned from processing short sales transfers to everything I do. You see, after you've worked short sales for a while, there is nothing you cannot accomplish. You get your way, and nobody messes with you. It's like you are on a warpath. Well, not actually a warpath—but don't mess with me.

Once, a few years back, when one of the juniors of the Zavala clan was completing his college applications, I had a question as to whether one of the science courses he had taken would be accepted to meet an admissions requirement.

The university website said yes; the high school guidance counselor said no.

But I've been a short sale negotiator. I push and push until I am 100 percent certain that the answer that I receive is accurate. Poor high school guidance counselor, she didn't know who she was up against. She was probably a little ticked that this particular parent was taking so much of her time, dealing with what she likely perceived to be a trivial issue.

That's the problem with short sales—you need to push and push and push. Unfortunately, some folks just don't have that kind of personality. There's a generalization (or stereotype) that all Californians are laid-back. But that's not the case for the agent who has successfully negotiated short sales for a living.

## It Takes Patience and Persistence to Multitask

Whether you are in California or Connecticut or anywhere in between, you need to be tenacious if you plan to successfully close more than one transaction at a time.

Top agents need to be able to manage multiple clients simultaneously. Depending upon the market, an agent's focus may move from buyers to sellers. But in general, high-producing agents prefer to manage lots and lots of listings because you can manage a lot more listings at one time than you can buyers.

When working with home buyers, you need to coordinate multiple property showings for all of your different buyers. Whereas when working with sellers, you concentrate on marketing the property for sale and let the buyers' agents handle showings.

However, one of the most common obstacles for agents is the fact that they cycle back to a single deal instead of managing multiple inputs.

It requires quite a bit of tenacity and persistence to be able to make phone calls and follow up on multiple transactions each and every day while, at the same time, prospecting and generating leads. But the key is to stick to it—day in and day out.

Because of all of the different tasks required, it's no wonder that many agents complain. If you do not have the patience of a saint or the relaxed nature of a stereotypical Californian and tenacity is not one of your superpowers, you may feel that there are days when you want to give up.

I didn't give up in seeking the answer to that university admission question, and I hope that I didn't embarrass my son in the process. I did learn that I was correct, and the course he had taken was a qualifying course. He was very happy because he didn't have to take another science class.

Like my grateful college-bound son, I know that any home buyers and home sellers that come my way are pleased that I am on a quest on their behalf—a quest that some may perceive as a "warpath."

## Can You Survive the Market Media Hype?

If you were a fly on the wall in my office, you'd probably be shocked at all of the questions I answer about distressed properties. I think it would also surprise you that much of my time is spent dispelling myths.

You know about myths, right?

Do you remember the one about the friend of a friend that went to Tijuana and brought back just about the most adorable Chihuahua that you have ever seen? Yet when the Chihuahua was not well, your friend of a friend brought it to the veterinarian—only to learn that the dog was actually a giant rat?

Or maybe you've heard the one about your friend of a friend who went back to her car after doing some grocery shopping. Seated in the backseat of her car, your friend of a friend found a sweet old lady who said she needed assistance. Lo and behold, your friend of a friend found out that this sweet old lady was actually a man dressed as an old woman and carrying a hatchet!

If you haven't heard these, then I am sure that you have heard other urban myths, and they stick. Boy, do they ever stick!

Inflated and misconstrued news information sticks just as well as an urban myth.

A few years back, someone heard on the news that there was a **moratorium** on foreclosures. He told a friend who was selling his home as a short sale not to bother with the sale because there was a moratorium on foreclosures.

Yet the most crucial detail, the one about the moratorium only lasting for ten days around the holidays, was forgotten or omitted. And as a result, this individual lost his home to foreclosure.

## Never Let the Spin Get You

I'm not trying to disparage news media, but very often, there is a lot more to a story than the thirty seconds devoted to it on national television.

In 2009, President Obama signed the American Recovery and Reinvestment Act. The loan modification program that was part of it (informally called **HAMP**) was touted as the answer to avoiding foreclosure for approximately four million borrowers.

Yet this program was completely inflated. Confused borrowers neglected to understand that they needed to be employed in order to qualify for a loan modification.

On the surface, this program was to help 4 million borrowers, yet four years later, only 1.25 million loan modifications had been completed. Plus, in 2013, 27 percent of borrowers had already redefaulted on those very same modifications.

What does an unrealistic spin—a less-than-thorough explanation of an ineffectual program—do to our national economy? It does the very same thing as the story about the Chihuahua or the old woman. It spreads untruths that people want to "buy" or believe in because they want to hold out hope.

## How to Handle Misinformation

Real estate agents need to be able to move forward and persist despite all of the misinformation that consumers may receive about programs and possibilities. Real estate professionals need to be there to answer the phone and dispel these myths by providing the truth and being prepared to support that truth with raw data.

How can individuals and small businesses compete with such a huge platform like the national media?

It's tough. But in order to succeed, you need to be prepared. You need to be able to provide counterevidence for any poorly reported story, and you need to be able to do so in a congenial manner.

Many home buyers and sellers have trouble understanding that real estate professionals provide something of value: we know the contracts, we know the neighborhoods, and we know the best way to get a home buyer or seller the best deal possible. And if we know all about the product at a local level, we can provide a lot more meaning than that ineffective news story.

But as salespeople, we often end up carrying the weight of the bad public image created by the rotten apples. As a result, our job can seem pretty tough sometimes.

It is a thrill to help a young couple buy their first home and then help them to buy a larger one after they have children. It is an amazing feeling to help a friend of a friend avoid foreclosure by means of a short sale. The folks that you meet along the way become lifelong friends.

For all of these reasons, I am able to get up every day and do my job. It doesn't matter whether one magazine or news station maligns the market or misinforms the public; I don't talk about rats and hatchets.

I can take all the media spin and convert my misinformed caller into a future home buyer, home seller, or prospective client.

The big question is . . . can you?

## Give It Your All

One night, while channel surfing, I came upon a program called *Kitchen Nightmares*. The premise is that Chef Gordon Ramsay goes out to a restaurant in order to rehabilitate it.

The show appears to follow the same format in each episode. Chef Ramsay redecorates, clears the place of rodents and dirt, changes the menu, and uses a tough love approach on the owners and the employees. At the end of the hour-long program, the new restaurant is a smashing success.

In the particular episode that I watched, Chef Ramsay asked one of the owners the following question: "When was the last time you gave 100 percent?" The owner responded by saying that he could not remember the last time that he put 100 percent of his effort into anything at all.

I immediately began to reflect on that question and the response. I could not, for the life of me, fathom the concept of not putting lots of effort into my work.

As real estate aficionados, we must put 100 percent of our effort into our transactions; it's the only way that we can generate new leads and complete contract negotiations.

We must take everything we do very seriously. We have someone's future in a file on our desk. Not taking that seriously would imply that we do not care about the future of others.

It's easy to put 100 percent of your effort into something that you love—your passion. Maybe it's running or bicycling. Maybe it's cooking (probably not for the restaurant owners on that episode of *Kitchen Nightmares*), or maybe it's real estate.

Famous author and marketing genius Gary Vaynerchuk says that it's more important to focus on your passion than it is to chase the dollars. When you have passion for what you do, then you might work long hours—and not even call it work.

Not sure that I would stay up until 2:00 a.m. calling bank employees, but I have been known to call the lenders at the crack of dawn while still in my jammies. When I have a client that requires a little extra something, I certainly put in the effort, and that persistence has led to success and lifelong referrals.

# LEARN TO EARN
## The Principle of Professional Development

When it comes to real estate, knowledge is power. Product knowledge—knowing your communities, properties available for sale, local architecture, floor plans, and available loan programs—can mean more sales.

It is difficult to effectively sell to a prospective home buyer or take a property listing if you cannot adequately address a potential client's needs.

There are many benefits to being a real estate professional that knows his or her product. Those with significant product knowledge have stronger communication skills and increased confidence and enthusiasm.

When you are comfortable and confident in providing the correct information to buyers and sellers, that confidence and product knowledge will pay off in improved sales results.

### Why Does Learning New Things Matter?

When I was a little girl, we didn't have a swimming pool. During those hot Southern California summers, sometimes we were lucky enough to be invited to the cousins' pool—a huge rectangular thing with a diving board. It was a child's dream, and we were always so excited when we got that invitation.

Generally, when we went to the cousins' pool, there were other families that were also invited—families that didn't have pools but had kids who needed entertaining. Those parents were probably just as desirous of the opportunity to get their kids out of the house as my own folks—exercise and entertainment and absolutely free!

After one of those swimming days, I remember that my mother made a comment about another mother at the pool. Apparently, this other woman stated that she hated learning new things. My mother next said that she must've misunderstood the comment because it just didn't make sense.

As an eight-year-old girl, I didn't really understand what my mother was saying. Who cares whether adults don't like to learn new things? Why did this upset my mother so much? As a young kid, I assumed that adults knew everything. Why did they need to learn anything new?

I dismissed this episode until I began contemplating the importance of competence and product knowledge when mastering your craft.

Having worked with countless real estate professionals, I can honestly say that the ones that always get the listings are the ones that like learning new things and who know their product.

As an adult, I now understand why it was so important to my mother that people care about learning new things.

## Gain Product Knowledge and Competence

It doesn't matter whether the product is the economy, the latest local property listings, or the newest policies and procedures with respect to distressed properties.

To be successful, you must love learning new things. You must master them with passion. You must be able to convey that passion and that knowledge when working with your clients.

### Way No. 1: *Attend local marketing sessions where available.*

Brand-new agents and seasoned agents alike can gain product knowledge at the local marketing sessions (also called the broker caravan or broker open). Local real estate boards and associations arrange these meetings and caravans so that agents can advertise their property listings, hold open houses, and share important industry news.

For new agents, these meetings are vital to obtaining product knowledge.

Generally, after the meetings, many agents will hold their homes open for agents to tour. Any agent worth his salt will take the time to go out and see each and every property that is open.

Agents often ask me why they should preview these properties when they do not have a buyer looking for a home with those particular specifications. But the truth is that it is a no-brainer.

### Become a Neighborhood Expert

If, over the course of a year or two, you tour five homes per week, you will have seen a large sampling of homes in your area. You will know the floor plans of the homes in many of the communities in your city. Then when you get a listing call in a certain area, you will immediately know the style and floor plan of that home—before you have even seen it.

Without even previewing that specific home, you will be able to speak as a neighborhood expert. And that's a great way to display product knowledge.

For new and seasoned agents, the agent tour and meeting also serves as a valuable way to network, share ideas, and learn about market conditions. Knowing what homes are **pocket listings**, new to the market, or coming soon to your area helps you stand out in the crowd.

**Way No. 2:** *Start using feed readers.*

If you have not already become acquainted, let me introduce you
to the concept of a feed reader. A feed reader is an online platform
for reading RSS feeds. Most blogs and news outlets share their
articles via an RSS feed.

It is important for agents to be knowledgeable about the current
conditions of the market. Yet it would be virtually impossible for an
agent to spend several hours each day searching the Internet and
going from website to website to read important real estate articles.
That's where RSS feed readers can help.

### Make It Easy on Yourself

RSS feed readers will pull all of your favorite RSS feeds into one
place, where you can peruse headlines and check out articles at the
drop of a hat. Not only will you save time when using a feed reader,
but you will also read more and become more knowledgeable.

**Way No. 3:** *Listen to news radio.*

As a real estate agent, you put a lot of mileage on your car. A
lot. What do you do in your car when you are driving from place to
place? Do you listen to music? Have you ever considered the car to
be the perfect place to gain product knowledge?

Listening to news radio and keeping up to date on the latest real
estate news while driving is a simple and easy way to increase or
maintain product knowledge.

### Use Your Drive Time to Impress

There have been countless times over the years when I have
heard some statistic about unemployment or housing on the radio
while on my way to a speaking engagement and then shared the
very same statistic during the speaking engagement. It's impressive,
people notice it, and it is easy to do. Just turn on the radio and listen.

Satellite radio is one tool that improves the news radio experience. It works wherever you are, and you have a wide variety of

national news channels available. If you can afford satellite radio, you may want to make an investment.

Don't forget that educating yourself—even in the car—could be considered continuing education. Check in with your accountant or tax attorney to see how you can maximize your deductions when you use your drive time to impress.

### Way No. 4: *Attend workshops and webinars.*

Even if you are not going out for any special designation, you may want to attend some of the free and low-cost online webinars or workshops available in your area. What a great way to learn new things and also maintain awareness of the changes that occur in the real estate industry!

Your local real estate board may offer classes on property management, short sales, technology, risk management, contracts, forms, and state laws—all things that you need in order to enhance your product knowledge and do your job well.

## Sharing Is Caring

Once you have product knowledge, share what you know. One of the best and most cost-effective methods for sharing your knowledge is through the Internet.

A total of 90 percent of home buyers and home sellers begin their home search on the Internet. So you have got to be there to be seen. And one of the best ways to share your product knowledge and increase your credibility is with a blog.

A well-crafted blog post with high-quality search engine optimization can lead to more buyer and seller leads than you can imagine.

I cannot count the number of times that I have received a call from sellers that I have never met before because of my blog. The sellers usually tell me that they would like me to come to their home and list their property. No competition. No fancy listing presentation. I go. They sign.

Since I have already demonstrated my competence and product knowledge online, I don't need to sell prospects on some fancy red convertible with all the bells and whistles. The blog has proven to them that I am a trusted professional; they have already done their research, and they have chosen me.

You can achieve the very same success in your real estate career. And you can begin to achieve that success through product knowledge, professional development, and a demonstrated passion for learning new things.

## ADVICE FROM THE FRONT LINE

### What's Included in the Short Sale Package?

Whether you are a listing agent negotiating a short sale or a seller getting ready to venture down the short sale road, it is important to know what is required by the lender in order to process a short sale.

First off, banks will always require a complete short sale package. If you do not submit everything on this list, you will not get very far.

When collecting and preparing documents, know that it is always best to submit the complete package to the lender the first time—doing so will save you hours and a big headache later on.

I've provided a list of what needs to be included in the short sale package. Note that the list of required items rarely varies from lender to lender, but some lenders may have their own branded versions of the forms on this list.

- Third-party authorization
- Financial statement
- Hardship letter
- Two months of bank statements
- Two years of tax returns

- Two recent pay stubs
- Listing agreement
- **Purchase contract**
- **Estimated settlement statement (HUD-1)**

It can be difficult to pull together this package, especially if you have many borrowers, since all of the financial documents are required for each borrower named on the loan.

However, I guarantee that if you send the short sale package to the lender correctly the first time, you will save yourself from a world of trouble down the road!

## *Don't Start to Dance Just Yet*

If you are an agent who has worked the distressed property market, you have, no doubt, realized that you are very unique! You were able to discover a niche and ride with it. That's a special talent.

If you haven't gotten a lienholder or short sale approval letter yet or if you have only gotten a few, there are some things that you need to know.

Obtaining approval letters is stressful. Obtaining approval letters takes time—sometimes so much time that everything else on your schedule goes by the wayside. Sometimes we have to beg, plead, or practically offer our firstborn in exchange for the approval letter.

Sometimes that letter just comes through the fax machine unannounced.

No matter how you get your approval letter, one thing is for sure: you must check and double-check all the details of that letter immediately upon receipt. Never assume that the letter is correct—that it has the correct name of the buyer or the seller, that it has the correct loan number or correct net amount due to the lender.

You must carefully check all of these details before moving

forward. These letters frequently contain errors, so your attention to detail and your product knowledge are vital at this stage of the game.

Every time—every single time—I receive an approval letter, I do a happy dance. You work so hard to obtain the letter that you just want to dance when it finally shows up. I've done a lot of happy dances—well over 1,500 of them.

Nevertheless, sometimes I do not heed my own warnings immediately. Then a little bit later, I sit down and check out the letter—only to find an error or a correction that needs to be made.

## Hold Your Horses, You Are Short to Close

As agents, we haven't spent too much of our careers scrutinizing estimated closing statements. We usually leave that work to escrow officers or settlement agents.

Unfortunately, with short sales, these statements are significantly more important in the early stages of the transaction than they used to be.

Why? That's because the banks request this document as part of the short sale package. The short sale lienholders want to see their bottom line. How much money are they going to net? How many cents on the dollar will they be forgiving?

Preparing the HUD-1 for the seller's first and second lienholders is truly an art form. This is primarily because mathematical calculations need to be done in order to assure that there is no funds shortage at closing.

Since it is difficult to determine how long the bank is going to take to approve the short sale, miscalculating the fees is not uncommon. It is also fairly common to forget to put all of the fees on the estimated settlement statement.

Sadly, this mistake could potentially blow the deal or, at the very minimum, cut into the agent's commission.

Because short sale deals are tricky and time-consuming, no agent wants the deal to go south, and no agent wants to give away any commission to cover seller costs not approved by the short sale lender.

In order to protect yourself, it is absolutely necessary to prepare the HUD-1 and make calculations based upon a closing date that is realistic. This way, taxes and any penalties will be calculated to a realistic date and not a date only a few weeks out.

Another key to accurate calculations is a careful review of the purchase contract. Did you allocate money for pest control, home-owner's association fees, potential liens, and any other fees?

While it was probably never your intention to get into the settle-ment component of the real estate transaction, can you imagine how much more knowledgeable we will all be . . . and can you imagine how much more appreciative we will be of our fellow escrow and settlement officers when short sales are behind us?

Knowledge of how the settlement statement works and why it is important to your short sale is vital when working in the field of distressed properties.

The truth is that the knowledge that you gained working short sales is product knowledge that stays with you. It can help you to address new and challenging real estate problems that come your way—even after the distressed property market is long gone.

## ADVANCING TO NEW TERRAIN

### *Competence Leads to Insights*

Being competent is crucial not only in real estate but in all things. One way that competence is demonstrated is in your ability to not only improve your skills but also to have deeper insights.

Take the case of negotiation. People always want my opinion as to whether the short sale transaction has gotten easier to negotiate throughout the course of this latest recession. It's a good question, and it is certainly something to ponder.

My product and market knowledge allows me to examine the big picture in ways that a less competent professional cannot. That skill can be very helpful because seeing a complex picture clearly is at least half the challenge. Having insights into that complex picture is even more helpful.

On the one hand, banks now have more than one individual working in their loss mitigation departments. Most banks have large loss mitigation departments, and many of those departments have multiple tiers of employees—each specializing in a certain aspect of the short sale negotiation process.

Additionally, banks such as Chase and Bank of America have gone as far as to invest big bucks in large automated systems to increase productivity.

On the other hand, some of the problems plaguing short sales transactions still exist. For example, many lending institutions are still slow to respond. Often, the employees are assigned to tasks for which they may be poorly qualified or untrained.

The lack of competence in the lending arena truly complicates the picture, making it harder to conduct effective transactions. A skilled professional sees the pitfalls and knows what to do to work around them. Competence literally pays dividends.

Beyond the distressed property arena, competence and product knowledge are vital. As a result of the mortgage meltdown, many borrowers stopped making their payments—not only mortgage payments, but other regular payments as well.

One area that has been hit particularly hard is the homeowner's association. With limited funds, some borrowers may have continued to pay their mortgages but defaulted on HOA monthly dues. Others may have ceased payments of both the HOA and the mortgage. As a result, many associations are now facing tough times.

Mortgage lenders are very cautious, and many refuse to make loans for borrowers purchasing homes or condominiums in areas where the association is in default or where there is a high delinquency rate.

Agents who are knowledgeable about these sorts of problems actually see increased closings. That's because they can anticipate a problem before it exists and avoid it.

For example, top agents may discourage borrowers obtaining certain types of loans from writing offers on condominiums in complexes where delinquency or default is a known problem.

In these examples, I'm sure that you can see how a little bit of knowledge can increase efficiency, productivity, and closed sales.

Developing this type of product knowledge is often the key to more closed transactions. That's why it's so important to be a person who is passionate about learning new things.

## Why Is Professional Development So Important?

For most real estate professionals, the business ebbs and flows with the seasons. Because of this, there are certain times of the year when it's easy to ignore professional development opportunities.

That's because you're earning money.

If you are seeing regular real estate closings, why would you want to improve your skills or increase your product knowledge, especially when that stuff is not required for state licensing?

Believe it or not, making an effort to grow professionally and increase your product knowledge will help you to be more successful and see regular closings instead of sporadic ones. If you are a person that doesn't like to learn new things, you may very well fall behind your competition, which could clearly be detrimental to your career.

There are countless professionals and industry leaders who can attest to the fact that you need to continually be reinventing yourself if you plan to succeed in real estate and beyond.

In this technology-focused real estate industry, you have to always be looking ahead to make sure that your skills are going to be marketable in the next five years.

You need to consider what you believe the industry will demand of you in the years to come, and you need to prepare yourself for those demands through professional development and product knowledge.

Since many companies offer brokerage models with limited professional development, it increasingly becomes the responsibility of the agent to take control of his or her own learning.

## Eight Ways to Grow Professionally

### Growth Tip No. 1: *Take a course.*

Just because you're no longer in school doesn't mean that classes are off-limits. Plenty of colleges offer courses and programs for adults, often in the evening so you can attend around your schedule.

As previously mentioned, other available options include online coursework and classes held at the local real estate association. Take a class on a topic that's relevant to what you're doing, or learn about something that can help you enter a new niche or prepare for coming changes to the industry.

### Growth Tip No. 2: *Teach yourself something new.*

You don't always need to take a class from a local college or real estate board to learn something new. Identify skills that are considered desirable, and start teaching yourself something new.

Search engine optimization, video editing, blogging, or other social media skills are a perfect example of things you can learn. Jump into a project, and learn the ropes as you go.

**Growth Tip No. 3: *Master an online tool.***

Even those of us who love technology don't always make the most of it. The Internet is full of free video tutorials on how to use all sorts of tools, including social media sites and business productivity tools.

Think about how you can increase your efficiency, and find Internet resources to help you accomplish that.

**Growth Tip No. 4: *Shadow another agent.***

Find workers within your brokerage who do something you want to learn, and ask them questions about what they do and how they do it. You don't need an official program to learn from others. All you need is initiative.

You can learn quite a bit by being a silent partner and sitting in at listing appointments or property showings of more experienced colleagues.

**Growth Tip No. 5: *Find a mentor.***

Identify people that you know that are willing to give you support and guidance. For agents, this is generally a top producer or veteran agent with loads of experience.

Even if you don't feel comfortable officially calling someone your mentor, having an individual to run ideas by who has more experience than you can go a long way toward learning how to be the best agent you can be.

The key here is that the individual you selected has to be interested in helping you, and sometimes those in the field of real estate are very competitive.

**Growth Tip No. 6: *Read.***

Read books, articles, and blogs within your niche. It's also fun to read things that are outside of real estate and consider how what you've read applies to the field of real estate.

### Growth Tip No. 7: *Attend a conference.*

Figure out which conference is most worthwhile to you, and make arrangements to attend. Not only will you learn new skills, but you'll also meet new people.

With so many national real estate networks, it's easy to research those attending and connect with them via social media before the event. Oftentimes, there are meet-ups and networking opportunities at the conference.

### Growth Tip No. 8: *Hone your skills.*

Most of us are aware of our weaknesses. Maybe we need to be better at meeting deadlines, or perhaps we need to get more organized.

Putting effort into improving your weaker skills will make you more marketable whether you are a newbie or a veteran agent. With the real estate industry being so tied to politics, the economy, and technological advances, it's one industry where you need to be constantly learning new things and embracing new ways to do the same old stuff.

You need to be thinking ahead as the latest, greatest way to do something may be right around the corner. Unfortunately, if you don't keep up, you may miss out on sales opportunities in your area.

## Has Anyone Ever Tried to Sell You a Bridge?

On the weekend, I often listen to Clark Howard on CNN via satellite radio. (I already told you that I'm a news radio junkie.) Listening to news programs in the car really does a number on my ability to increase my productivity. It also helps me to keep up with the latest news, even when I don't have time to check out the daily newspaper.

Clark Howard is a money guy and consumer advocate who provides tips and tools on how to be a savvy consumer, make good investment choices, and repair financial problems at any scale.

I recall that, once, Howard shared a scenario that had just played out in his own life. When he arrived home, a car was parked in front of his house. The individual in the auto had just purchased it from someone else via Craigslist, and the car had already broken down even before the buyer had made it home!

Most readers already know that it is important to be aware of potential fraud, especially when making purchases from buyers they do not know. But Howard's anecdote also brings to light the topic of credibility.

## Credibility Through Quality, Not Quantity

I often receive calls related to credibility. I receive calls from prospective sellers who are planning to list their homes with San Diego agents that employ my short sale negotiation services.

These sellers want to look into the credibility of the agents they had been planning to employ. These sellers also want to make sure I am *legit* and credible myself.

Kudos to them! If you are going to hire someone to help you sell one of the most valuable items you have ever owned, you might as well be sure that you hire someone who is credible.

I also receive calls from other agents seeking advice. Often, these agents express concern about the individual representing the other side of the transaction and whether that individual might not be credible or might be unscrupulous.

Realtors® all subscribe to a higher code of ethics. At least that's what they say is supposed to happen. But how can and how should consumers judge our credibility?

Is the agent who sends the most mailers the most credible? Is the one who has the most signs in the neighborhood or the most radio advertisements better equipped to negotiate a short sale or find a buyer than the agent who has a few less listings?

To that end, is the individual with the most blog posts more credible than the local agent who has only written a few blog posts? And why is it that the agent with more ads and more mailings is invited to speak to congressional panels in Washington, DC, when local agents who may be more representative of the majority are not invited?

As you move forward, consider how you can demonstrate credibility through your advertising, your product knowledge, and your public image. It's important to know the difference between just a good image and actually being a great agent.

Expertise isn't just for show. Demonstrating your integrity, not just bragging about it, is a huge piece of building a reputation of competence. You have to talk your talk and walk your walk.

Tips and tools relating to the information provided in this chapter can be found on the *Been There, Done That* resource page at www.melissazavala.com

# 5

# USE YOUR HEAD
## The Principle of Ingenuity

Using your head suggests that you consider an unconventional or new perspective. It refers to a state of mind that helps when trying to figure out a solution to a problem. Albeit cliché, using your head refers to thinking outside the box—looking at something in such a way that you turn it upside down in order to come up with a new strategy or solution.

While it may seem silly, agents gifted in seeking unconventional solutions often solve difficult problems and, as a result, see increased sales.

One excellent example of innovative thinking comes from the world of sports. In 1968, a high jumper named Dick Fosbury, who we will talk about at length a bit later, jumped higher over the bar than anyone had before—and that's because he went over back first, which was a new way to conquer the high jump.

Unconventional thinkers like Fosbury are open to new ideas. They are able to look at things from a different perspective and often take risks. This does not mean that the old ways of doing things are wrong; it simply means that it might be time to try something different.

When it comes to real estate, all sorts of problems can arise during a transaction. Among the problems that may occur are financial hurdles, boundary issues, or structural defects, all of which may get in the way of a smooth and easy closing.

When you can take a different perspective or think of a new and innovative solution to a conventional problem, you will see more quick and efficient real estate closings.

## Conventional and Unconventional Thinking

Around 2001, after hearing people ooh and aah about Robert Kiyosaki's *Rich Dad, Poor Dad*, I decided to read the book. I wanted to know what the hype was all about.

Kiyosaki advocates financial independence and building wealth through real estate investing, business development, and fiscal intelligence. He uses examples of his own father (the poor dad), who spends much of his time in school and in the rat race, and a family friend (the rich dad), whose entrepreneurial and enterprising can-do attitude leads to significantly more financial success.

I was born and raised with the "poor dad" mind-set. I have an advanced degree and loads of education. Despite the fact that I was taught to think for myself, I wasn't really taught entrepreneurial thinking—to think outside the box. I was encouraged to grow up and get a good job where I would report to someone else and earn a respectable salary.

The man I married, on the other hand, was raised outside the United States in a country where the only way to get ahead is by owning your own business. In that culture, being entrepreneurial, having business acumen, and using strategic and creative thinking are principal attributes of success. That mind-set has worked very well for him.

These starkly different approaches have helped me to see that being enterprising and challenging the corporate construct is not always a bad thing—when it is done delicately.

## Conduct Due Diligence

When I take a short sale listing or any listing, for that matter, I always conduct a slew of due diligence activities. Most notably, with the help of my friends in the title industry, I study a **preliminary title report**.

Who are the owners of the property? Are they the individuals that contacted me for the appointment or consultation? Is the property owned by a trust? Is there anything that could cause a cloud on the title, such as a tax lien or a city or county citation of some sort? Are there any other liens on the property? Is there the possibility that this property is a short sale or could end up in foreclosure?

When you conduct due diligence activities and ask questions like these early in the home-selling process, you have time to solve problems that could hamper the closing—issues for which creative and strategic thinking may be involved.

## A Look Inside the Lender's Box

I've often had to make strategic decisions with respect to short sales, especially in situations where the foreclosure date is just around the corner.

Instead of following all of the black-and-white rules exactly as they are dictated to me, I have delicately worked within the corporate construct to effectively and ethically get my way. It's a balance that needs to be respected.

As much as I love closing short sales, kicking the line too hard or too often can really backfire. You have to know the limits as you are working *inside the lender's box* to get your "box" deal done.

You may not realize it, but you probably already have experience working "inside the lender's box." For example, when a foreclosure auction date is about a week or two away, you may find that the short sale lender suddenly provides a **counteroffer** and wants to hurry things along because the lender needs to meet specific deadlines.

It's possible that the buyer does not agree to the terms of the counteroffer or the property value is a little bit off the mark.

However, you need to consider whether you should contest the value now—knowing that there is a risk that the lender will go ahead and foreclose if you do not agree. Or should you agree with the lender's terms, then consider arguing the price after the auction date has been postponed?

As a listing agent, I have a fiduciary obligation to the seller to do what is in the seller's best interest. So if the seller wants to avoid foreclosure, then I need to do what I can to work within the bank's deadlines and guidelines and get my job done at the same time.

It's my job to get the buyer's offer approved by the short sale lender and to get the transaction closed before the foreclosure date. For this reason, carefully thinking through the ramifications of any decision that comes out of my mouth is extremely important.

I try to avoid reacting immediately (or overreacting) even when a foreclosure date is around the corner. Although I may be forced into taking a specific action, I have a better chance of being effective if I make deliberate decisions rather than rushed or uncalculated ones.

## *Boost Strategic Thinking: Three Hot Tips*

Since creative and strategic thinking involves turning traditional perspectives upside down, it's important to start with an open mind. These are three great tips for enhancing your ability to think in new and innovative ways:

**Hot Tip No. 1: *Think before you speak.***

Even if you are very gifted at thinking on your feet, when you have someone's purchase or sale (or even their foreclosure) in the palm of your hands, you had better not screw it up.

It's always best not to make a snap decision but to consult others (your clients or even just your pillow) before risking a deal going sour. List the pros and cons, and make a decision that will work to your client's advantage.

### Hot Tip No. 2: *Don't burn your bridges.*

You will never ever achieve your goals if you complain about bank employees, your clients, or other agents.

Even when I am speaking with a bank executive and I know that a specific employee has been ineffective or a complete jerk, I merely state what I need in an objective manner. You never know when you will work with that individual again, and getting blacklisted is not a good thing.

When you are objective, you foster professional relationships that you can leverage in the future.

### Hot Tip No. 3: *Ask questions, and listen carefully.*

The best way to hatch a plan is to ask questions and listen carefully to the answers. For example, short sale lenders have specific rules and guidelines, and oftentimes, they will not deviate from those rules and guidelines. When speaking with a short sale lender, ask questions about those specific rules and guidelines, and then listen carefully to the answers.

Only when you understand why a short sale was declined or what the bank needs to see in order to approve the short sale can you adequately go back and restructure your short sale package in order to meet those guidelines. And you can apply this same method to just about any problem on your plate.

The more you are able to be flexible, innovative, and resourceful, the more successful you will be not only when working the distressed property market but in all things real estate and beyond.

---

## ADVICE FROM THE FRONT LINE

---

### *How to Avoid Real Estate Suicide*

I read an article on the Internet where the writer, also a short sale expert, was telling a story about some mishap in a real estate transaction. In the article, this writer used the saying "You have to choose the hill on which you want to die."

I'd never heard that saying before and was curious about where it came from. So I did a bit of research, and here is what I found:

> *A critical decision for any leader is to know which hills you are prepared to die on and to know you can't die on all of them. Making your choices about what is core to your own code is the first step toward being liberated to do what you must. Then you can live.*
>
> —Paul D. Houston

I was fascinated with this saying and how it seems to speak directly to real estate agents, especially those working short sales. It takes a lot to keep your cool when processing a short sale transaction. As you've already read, I once faxed the same short sale package to Litton Loan Servicing nine times over a period of five weeks and had confirmation that it went through each and every time. Yet the customer service folks said that they didn't have it.

Was I going to die on that hill? Was I going to scream, yell, and ruin my professional name because they couldn't find my package? Or would it be better to select an alternate strategy for getting over the hill?

I've seen many agents "die on the hill."

The key to success in real estate is that you cannot—you must not—ever lose your cool, no matter how stressful things become, no matter how irritated you are. I've had people swear at me, threaten me, and send me nasty e-mails. Nevertheless, I just ignore them, although I would prefer to respond in an impertinent manner.

I know that the tables will turn someday, and I do not want to risk burning a bridge that I may need to pass someday in the future. In real estate, instead of dying on the hill, why not look for another hill to climb—a different one that may actually lead you to the top?

Keep that in mind that the next time you want to give up or blow a gasket over something. Instead, you need to breathe in and breathe out. Do what you need to do in order to get around, above, and beyond the problem. Do yoga; eat chocolate cake. I don't care. No matter what, believe me that you would rather pass someone else's remains on your way up the hill than be a cadaver along the way.

## If You Want to Make Money, You Must Think Big

Do you remember Wimpy from the old Popeye cartoons? He was always looking at what was in it for him. If you remember Wimpy, then you remember that he used to say, "I'll gladly pay you Tuesday for a hamburger today."

The clear and obvious bottom line was that Wimpy wanted Popeye or the other characters to lend him money to purchase a burger, yet the implied message was that he would probably never pay them back. The burger was what was in it for Wimpy, and he was fiscally irresponsible.

As real estate agents, what is in it for us? Commission, of course, and lifelong referrals if we do a good job. Sometimes, however, the deal does not close, or we do not make much commission, yet we still have the opportunity for future referrals if we provide excellent customer service and have stellar people skills.

Helping someone sell or buy their largest asset or liability (even if the deal never closes) can go a long way toward establishing future business relationships.

## Would You Jeopardize a Deal?

Once, very early in my short sale career, I negotiated a deal where the second lienholder was holding out, and the only way we were going to be able to get the deal done was if we found an additional $4,000 to pay the second lienholder.

After trying everything under the sun to get the second lienholder to budge, I decided to call the listing agent. Maybe the buyer would be willing to kick in the $2,000? Maybe the seller would be willing to kick in the $2,000? Maybe everyone could throw in a little bit? Heck, if the seller really has no money and does not want to see his property go to foreclosure, I would help if I could.[1]

So I gave the listing agent a call. I explained the situation, and he said that he would rather see the property go to foreclosure than throw in any money.

I call myself a Realtor®, I call myself a broker, and I call myself a Short Sale Expeditor. I do not generally call myself a Commission Give Awayer. At the end of the day, if I have a choice between earning $10,000 in thirty days or nothing, I would pick the $10,000 every day of the week, every month of the year—especially if it will help a client out of a jam.

This listing agent was only looking for hamburgers today, not lifelong referrals tomorrow. He was missing out on the big secret: that the short sale is a way to grow your real estate business and fuel your real estate career for years to come.

If you want to be big, you have to think big and sometimes consider unconventional options. Big means not just the hamburger today, but the entire restaurant tomorrow.

---

[1] *If any party to the transaction makes a financial contribution that aids in the ability to close the transaction, this financial help must be disclosed on the HUD-1, which is supplied to the lienholders for final approval. Also, if the buyer is helping in any way, the buyer's lender must also be aware of this contribution. Nondisclosure could be a RESPA violation.*

## ADVANCING TO NEW TERRAIN

### *Navigating a Strategic Career Makeover*

My husband, a top-producing agent in his own right, came back from a meeting in 2010 and informed me that, during the meeting, the following statistic was reported: the average number of annual closed transactions for an agent in San Diego County was five. That's five per year!

I was surprised to hear that the number was so low. Depending upon where you live, the average sales price for a single-family residence could be anywhere from $100,000 to over $1 million. At the time of publication of this book, parts of Florida, Michigan, Ohio, and several other areas of the United States have home values that are under $100,000.

But what struck me as even more shocking than this number was that some major players in San Diego County who had previously closed many, many transactions were also closing near that average of five.

What happened? Well, I know already that the market happened. These agents didn't close their deals. But something else happened as well. These former real estate superstars did not reinvent themselves when the market changed. They did not break out of their box.

Business articles across the Internet state that the average individual needs to reinvent himself every five years. In real estate, I'd be willing to wager that you need to reinvent yourself a little more often than that.

### What Does It Mean *to Reinvent* Oneself?

To reinvent yourself does not mean that you need to change careers. Reinventing yourself means taking thoughtful strategic steps to change the way you do things so that your activities address changing demands of the marketplace.

If your real estate career isn't going the way that you hoped it would, it may be time to step away from some old strategies and move toward some new ones.

The real question is this: what do you want your life to look like?

The first step toward changing the direction of your real estate career is to figure out where you want to go.

Write down your thoughts. What do you want your career to look like? How much do you want to earn? How many hours per week do you want to work? Do you want to work harder or more efficiently? How do you want to contribute to the field of real estate on a grander scale?

Put aside your notes for a few days, and let them sink in. Visualize what your life would look like if you accomplished each one of the ideas that you noted. Then pull out your list again, and start setting the goals needed to support your change.

I have met and exceeded my past personal and professional goals over and over again because I have been continually reinventing myself for the last several years. When things change, I change too. I consider hurdles such as the mortgage meltdown to be bumps in the road. I drive over them and move on.

You can do the same thing. Just apply some creative strategic thinking to your career and your life, and you will find your way.

## Transition Your Business by Being Remarkable

Several years ago, while decompressing after my busy weekend, I was watching a few programs on television. My mind was wandering, and I heard the word "blackberry" within the context of the program. The wife said to the husband that she didn't want "blackberries" in the house.

Admittedly, I wasn't focused on the television program. But I could not understand why she was objecting to fruit in the house. It probably took me a full five seconds to realize that she was talking about the BlackBerry—the now-outdated smartphone, not the fruit.

Perhaps I couldn't make the switch in my head because I am a loyal iPhone user. But I also wonder why the BlackBerry has now become so unremarkable that the word didn't even conjure up an image of a smartphone.

## Do You Have a Purple Cow?

In *Purple Cow: Transform Your Business by Being Remarkable*, Seth Godin has an interesting take on being remarkable.

The premise—where the purple cow concept came from—is that if you are driving in your car and looking out the window, you may see some white and brown cows. You will gawk at them for a few moments, and then you will move on to something else.

But if you were ever to see a purple cow—something very different and exciting—you might remember it forever.

Transitioning this concept to your business, how can you be a purple cow—something that is different and exciting, something or someone that people will remember forever?

## What Makes You So Special?

As agents, we certainly want to be remarkable. We want to demonstrate remarkable behavior so that we get repeat business for years and years to come. We have to learn to think strategically, in different ways than we have before, to uncover the remarkable things that are hidden within us.

Remarkable stuff can be in our packaging—our business cards, our signs, and our presentation. Maybe even the car we drive can help to brand us as the purple cow of our real estate community.

Remarkable can also be in our demeanor and in how we conduct business. And here is where it gets tricky. Godin says, "Remarkable isn't always about changing the biggest machine in the factory. It can be the way you answer the phone, launch a new brand, or price a revision of your software."

As agents, what do you do that is remarkable? What do you do that sets you apart and makes you a purple cow?

One of the absolute easiest things that you can do is to take or return all phone calls immediately. I respond to all e-mails very, very quickly. Since I have heard plenty of complaints about agents who do not return calls, maybe that small intentional move will be enough to set me apart.

Perhaps you drive a red car, have a red business card, or wear red to all your appointments. People will remember you when you do things that are memorable or remarkable.

Being remarkable needs to be included in your strategy. Find your purple cow.

## Will Your Job Be Eliminated?

Seth Godin not only talks about cows, but he shares marketing ideas and thoughts about how to rethink your business. Generally, his audience is the entrepreneur or the small-business person, and occasionally, he specifically mentions real estate agents.

Godin refers to agents in this passage when he speaks about the information age and the quantity and volume of information that the hoi polloi can gather just from surfing the Internet. He states,

> *The minute real estate listings went online was the minute that it was no longer sufficient that a real estate broker merely had information about real estate listings . . . Information is in a hurry to flow, and if someone comes up with a better, more direct, faster*

*and cheaper way for information to get from one place to another,*
*they will eliminate your [the real estate agent's] reason for being.*

—Seth Godin

Realtors®, don't take his comments personally despite the fact that he
may be talking about you.

What he means here is that long, long gone are the days when
people would call you for a list of homes for sale or a free comparative market analysis.

So what's next? What is the future for agents? Does it mean we
are doomed to failure? Or is Godin simply pointing out the challenges of competing in the future?

Almost every day of the week, you can read an online article
where someone moans about listing syndication, where they lament
their fate, and gripe about how the large syndication sites inhibit an
agent's unique ability to generate leads.

The general complaint is that the information is inaccurate and
that the spirit of syndication sites is detrimental to the success of the
local agent.

While I may eat my words someday, I currently cannot imagine
a time when we will be able to stop these large companies from
providing access to most of the homes available for sale.

What Godin suggests is that the way we compete is to consider
whether each of us provides enough "non-commodity service and
customization" that people will actually come to us for our service
anyway.

## Consider Your Strategic Options

One Texas real estate firm made the news in 2013 when they decided
that their website would not even bother to compete with the large
syndication companies. Since they know that they cannot compete,
they say, "Why bother?"

Fischer Real Estate Services in Fort Worth decided that they would take their business in a whole different direction. Despite the fact that almost every other brokerage has one, there is no home search on their brokerage website. Since Zillow, Trulia, and other large IDX syndicators dominate page 1 of the search engines, Fischer decided to remove itself from the field.

That's their approach. You need to rethink yours.

Recently, in my neck of the woods, a failing golf course was sold to a developer that wished to build hundreds of new homes.

Countless meetings have occurred to protest the development. There is no question that if you had a golf course view and now that was gone, you would be mighty mad.

That being said, as a real estate professional, I think that some agents would be pleased with the fact that inventory will increase. Big thinkers might consider this an opportunity to work with the developer on a joint venture—to become their listing and sales brokerage of choice.

While there is certainly something admirable about taking a stand, there comes a point where "you can't fight city hall." Godin states that it is the non-commodity service or customization that can help you attract leads despite the fact that there is always someone better, cheaper, and faster.

It's time to get strategic and really understand the value you bring to your clients and to the marketplace. Know it deep down inside, and lead with it. Clients need knowledge and wisdom, not just data or information. Give them that, and you will be unstoppable.

## If the Oakland A's Could Do It . . .

When we discussed professional development, we addressed reading nonbusiness materials—perhaps even fiction—and then relating what you learn from those materials to your business. You can do the same thing with films. For example, the movie *Moneyball* can really teach us a lot about thinking in atypical ways.

For those who are unfamiliar with the story line, Brad Pitt plays Billy Beane, a former professional baseball player and current general manager and minority owner of the Oakland A's.

The movie depicts the real-life challenges faced by this team when competing in a field with teams such as the New York Yankees that have budgets that are over three times greater than the budget of the Oakland A's.

What Beane realizes is that sometimes all teams cannot compete by the same rules. In cases such as this, what you have to do is to create a new way in which to gain success. You have to think strategically, and that is what he does.

In this unique and challenging real estate market, there are some agents who cannot see the forest for the trees. Instead of spewing gloom and doom, why not look into the outfield and see the home run you can hit when you market your services to people who need your help today?

People who need your help today may include the unemployed homeowner who cannot afford to sustain mortgage payments much longer, anyone who has missed two payments on their mortgage (statistics show that they will likely not recover), anyone who is working on a loan modification, and even those homeowners with views of a now-closed golf course.

If you haven't seen the movie yet, I would highly recommend it and would urge you to consider how using creative thinking like Billy Beane may take your real estate career to the next level.

Just remember, it's important to study things deeply and consider options. A strategic mind may not always help, but it certainly won't hurt. In fact, when you try new methods and solutions, you will likely see increased closings and win big—just like the Oakland A's.

Want to learn more about how to conduct a strategic makeover on your real estate business? Check out the *Been There, Done That* resource page at www.melissazavala.com to learn more.

# RESPECT THE ROUTINE
## The Principle of Commitment

Just because you are an independent contractor doesn't mean that you get to sit at home by the pool all day and soak up the sun. Being successful in real estate (or in pretty much anything) means that you have to be dedicated, disciplined, and persistent. You have to show up and keep plugging away each and every day of the week!

In my meetings with other agents, we often discuss what they are doing to generate new business.

I remember one gentleman in particular who was incredibly gifted at the art of gab. He told me that he had tried door knocking for listings and that it did not work.

While I fully recognize that door knocking is not for everyone, I asked him to tell me more, knowing full well that this guy could sell just about anything you put in front of him.

He related to me that he went out to a local neighborhood, fully prepared to meet people and make deals.

He parked his car, approached the first door, and knocked. The person who answered the door (presumably the homeowner) was not pleased with the disruption and shut the door. That was the end of that. "Door knocking doesn't work," he said.

## *Once Is Not Enough*

"Well, it sounds to me like you only tried it once. How can you be certain that it is not an effective tactic for obtaining listings?" I responded.

From the look on his face, I could tell that he really didn't appreciate my comment.

The best way to determine whether door knocking is effective for you is to go out a minimum of once a week for a period of three to six months. Knock on at least three to five doors each time you set out. Only after you have dedicated a fair amount of time to a task such as door knocking can you evaluate whether or not it will be a moneymaker or lead generator.

## *To Grow, You Must Work Your Plan*

Persistence and dedication are vital to success in real estate, and they are required components of success in the short sale world as well. These three practical tips will help you stay focused amid the many distractions faced by all of us.

**Tip No. 1:** *Create a preset schedule for your weekly activities.*

Research shows that time blocking can lead to increased productivity.

When you set out specific times each day to complete your paperwork or contact leads, you maintain focus, and your productivity increases. Use your smartphone or your daily planner to coordinate activities, and do not schedule appointments during time that has already been blocked for other things.

**Tip No. 2:** *Focus on process rather than outcome.*

Set your long-range goals, then list the daily, weekly, and monthly activities needed to meet those goals. Long-range goals are a product of your process.

It's best to focus on your process (the things you do on a regular basis) rather than the outcome. Create a calendar of concrete activities (social media marketing, cold calling, direct mailing), and strictly adhere to that calendar. Instead of fixating on things that are out of reach, practice a regular routine, and concentrate on mastering repeated processes.

### Tip No. 3: *Exert self-control.*

While easier said than done, if you note daily and weekly goals, commit to completing them. This may mean staying home on a Friday night or working on Saturday. The key is to stick to it. It's like going to the gym or dieting—once you skip a day, it's hard to get back on track.

Success in all things real estate involves consistency and dedication. It means demonstrating the self-discipline to show up and get it done—each and every day of the week.

## ADVICE FROM THE FRONT LINE

## *Twelve Habits of Top Short Sale Agents*

If you're a short sale superstar, then you are probably already familiar with the short sale process. Congratulations for having the dedication to conquer this difficult path.

No matter your current skill or experience level, if you are committed to sharpening your short sale skills and want to close more short sale deals in the future, here is a consolidated list of the twelve things you must know and do in order to get your short sale approved.

### Habit No. 1: *Understand available short sale incentive programs.*

When you know about the current programs available, you

are able to provide your clients with more detailed and insightful information so that they can make a more informed decision.

### Habit No. 2: *Collect all documents for the short sale package at the listing appointment.*

Some sellers feel anxious about the short sale of their home. If you collect the lender-required documents up front, you can provide your clients with a much more seamless (and less stressful) experience.

### Habit No. 3: *Collect the statement of information when the short sale listing is taken.*

In order to avoid working hard on a transaction that may never close, it is a good idea to learn about all of the liens associated with the sale at the very beginning of the process—since they all must be satisfied prior to closing. This can be done by having your clients complete a **statement of information**.

### Habit No. 4: *Order and read the preliminary title report.*

This report provides lots of information about the property, including details about mortgage liens and ownership. Check the document early in the process to ensure that you are working with the correct lenders and the correct owners.

### Habit No. 5: *Obtain repair and pest control estimates prior to submitting your short sale to the bank.*

When you obtain bids in advance, you can provide the mortgage lender with a complete picture of the property and any related maintenance issues.

### Habit No. 6: *Ensure that the settlement statement you submit to the bank has the correct figures for your closing date.*

Factor in every possible charge that may be associated with the sale, and estimate all per diem fees to a realistic closing date.

### Habit No. 7: *Submit a complete short sale package to the bank, and include a fully executed offer.*

When you send your paperwork piecemeal, the multiple faxes and e-mails may get lost or misplaced during the process. It's always best to send one package that includes all items.

### Habit No. 8: *Avoid using electronic signatures whenever possible.*

Some lenders do not permit electronic signatures on contracts and forms. Unless you are certain that your client's lender accepts electronic signatures, avoid them.

### Habit No. 9: *Maintain regular weekly communication with all parties during the negotiation process.*

Regular contact with all parties (including the seller and the buyer's agent) helps to ensure that everyone will be ready when the short sale approval arrives.

### Habit No. 10: *Make sure that the sellers have decided where they are going to live when the deal closes.*

Assist your sellers to prepare their exit strategy. Sellers need to be ready to relocate on or before the closing date.

### Habit No. 11: *Follow up regularly with the short sale lender.*

Your persistence and dedication to regular contact with the lender will ensure that the short sale closes more quickly and efficiently.

### Habit No. 12: *Whatever happens, maintain a positive attitude.*

Remember that you attract bees with honey, not vinegar. The parties to the transaction, including the mortgage lender, will appreciate your enthusiasm.

It doesn't matter what happens. It doesn't matter who bullies you or yells at you. It doesn't matter that you have already faxed the same item to the bank nine times. No matter what happens, if you continually work your transaction daily and maintain a positive attitude, the short sale will close—eventually.

## Dominate Your Niche Like a Rock Star

In a field such as real estate, the key to success is always changing. With a fluctuating economy, the marketplace is never stable. Top-producing real estate professionals are always entrenched in the market and hyperfocused on current trends.

To be the best that you can be, you can't skate on the knowledge of yesteryear or the skills you started with. That's where dedication comes in.

If you show up every day, then you are acutely aware of the subtle nuances of your profession or your niche; you can address issues accordingly and get your transactions closed more effectively.

Often, the secret is for you to simply keep plugging away, even as things change or as situations evolve.

Conduct a reality check, and keep doing what you know to be the right thing. However, last year's rules are not necessarily the rules today, and completing your daily tasks is often the answer to being in the know.

The busier and more active you are, the more tricks and tips you'll pick up along the way. That's why it is so important to show up every day; the simple act of completing daily activities will help lead to mastery.

### What Everybody Ought to Know About "Cash Is King"

Now and again, the topic of cash offers seems to come up, and the Internet is abuzz with people who reflect on the expression "Cash is king." In short sales, when writing an offer, many buyers and buyers' agents may perceive that the cash offer is "king" (the best offer on the table).

Receiving the title of king occurs in a variety of ways. For Elvis and for Michael Jackson, King was a title conferred upon them because they dominated their fields. For the royals, it is a title that comes with a birthright.

How exactly does a cash offer become "king"?

Established short sale agents know that there are some significant benefits to accepting a cash offer. For one, the cash buyer does not have to obtain a mortgage loan. This very fact can speed up the closing of the transaction.

Additionally, a cash buyer may have a little bit of wiggle room when and if the bank does not approve funds for certain items required for the short sale closing.

For example, if there are delinquent homeowner's association dues or an unpaid lien, the cash buyer might be able to contribute some funds to cover those fees.

Ultimately, in a pinch and if the foreclosure auction is imminent, the cash buyer can close more quickly. That last fact is often seen as a positive one by the short sale negotiators and processors at the bank.

## Cash Burns Holes in Pockets

Oftentimes, cash buyers (by the very nature of being cash buyers) are more fluid. Since these buyers do not require a loan, they can continue to look at properties or shop around.

Additionally, many cash buyers are investors that are looking for an investment with a strong return. So if the short sale lender requests slightly more money, the cash buyer might move on to another investment.

Note that, as an investor buyer, the cash buyer is not emotionally attached to the property the way a first-time home buyer might be. For example, a first-time home buyer might seek a specific school district or neighborhood, whereas the investor is often more focused on the financial bottom line.

## Do Short Sale Lenders Play Favorites?

With respect to short sale negotiations, few and far between are the times when bank employees will speed up their corporate time frames or take a lesser dollar amount because a cash buyer has submitted an offer.

If an investor, such as Fannie Mae or Freddie Mac, has done due diligence and decided upon a minimum net amount, the very fact that the offer is cash will not usually coerce the lender into accepting something less than the predetermined net amount.

Short sale lenders don't play favorites, and it is not often that a bank will speed things up when a cash offer is on the table.

I've gotten a few short sales approved in record time—several in under a week. However, in all of those cases, I already had a fully approved package in the hands of a higher-level executive who was just waiting for me to submit either a new offer or an offer that already met some predetermined or preapproved terms.

So in those cases, it might not have been the cash that was king; it may have been (like Elvis and Michael Jackson) a title conferred upon me because of my domination in the field.

Cash certainly may be of benefit when considering the purchase of a short sale. As to whether cash is king, it is important to have the market knowledge to address this issue when it comes your way. Clearly, that knowledge comes from hard work and self-discipline.

## Now You Can Have an Error-Free Transaction

When you are in it to win and you are working hard each day, it's always best not to make mistakes. We all make 'em, and sometimes these errors can be costly. An error on your part could cost your clients time and money; your clients could even lose out on an opportunity if you are not careful.

Some 90 percent of problems people have with their computers are due to operator or user error. That's a fairly significant number. It means that ninety out of every one hundred calls to technical support relate to a misunderstanding about the use of a product. Only 10 percent of calls relate to a flaw in the product.

Along those lines and applying that theory to short sales, it would stand to reason that 90 percent of the problems that people associate with short sale transactions are due to user error—to an error on the part of the buyer's agent, the buyer, the listing agent, the seller, or the mortgage lender.

Since there are so many people involved in a transaction, it's not surprising that 90 percent of the problems are due to small errors.

## Manage Buyer and Seller Expectations

One way to avoid errors and troubles within the short sale transaction is to manage seller expectations.

For a short sale seller, providing information and education would mean that the listing agent would be responsible for managing the seller's expectations—offering a timeline for the short sale transaction, setting out a best- and worst-case scenario, conducting due diligence activities to assure that the seller will qualify.

For the listing agent, user error can occur when a listing agent is in over his or her head. Not all negotiations are a walk in the park. Some are complicated and include two or three liens, unpaid homeowner's association dues, and significant property damage.

For the buyer and the buyer's agent, it is also important to manage expectations.

Buyers need to know what they are getting into when they write an offer on a short sale. They need to know how long the process may take, what the risks are, and that certain items that they have requested when writing their offer to purchase may not, in fact, be approved as part of the short sale process. Are the buyers willing to wait three months only to find out that termite damage repairs or a closing cost concession will not be approved?

Poorly managed expectations can lead to a botched transaction down the road.

## Short Sale Lenders May Make Mistakes

Operator or user error often occurs at the bank. I once had a short sale in my pipeline where all of the seller documentation was submitted through the online platform, but we were not getting any response from the short sale lender.

Thirty-seven phone calls and a million apologies had us back where we started. We were told that there was a "glitch in the system," and the lender would be closing the file and opening it anew.

Dealing with user error in the distressed property world takes patience and dedication. It requires paying attention to all the details to assure that nothing falls through the cracks.

To me, that means showing up and touching every file every single day. That's how you prove to your sellers, your colleagues, and the short sale lenders that you are in it to be successful.

## ADVANCING TO NEW TERRAIN

### *In Sports and Real Estate, Dedication Pays Off*

As you may already know, Dick Fosbury is one of the most influential athletes in track and field. That's because he revolutionized the high jump by inventing the back-first technique (known as the Fosbury flop) that has been adopted by jumpers today.

By altering the traditional way of jumping and consistently (and doggedly) working to perfect this new technique with relentless dedication, Fosbury was able to improve his jump height by almost eighteen inches in under three years! That's how he made sports history.

The same dedication can be applied to many aspects of the field of real estate, but most definitely with respect to lead generation.

## How to Find Short Sale Leads

So are you looking for leads? Do you want listings? In many parts of the United States, there may still be a shortage of housing inventory. Absorption rates in some parts of the United States are measured in days (as opposed to months), and agents are clamoring for more inventory—including short sale listings.

There are many ways to identify a possible short sale listing, the most common of which is to obtain a list of properties where the borrower is in active foreclosure and then pursue those borrowers through direct mail and other traditional marketing methods.

While there are lots of prospective sellers that need your help today, some may not know it yet. Consider how you can find these folks, and consider what items of value you can offer them in order to capture those leads.

## Practice the Rule of Eleven

About two decades ago, *Dateline* reported that in order to convince small children to eat vegetables such as broccoli or spinach, it is best to present those vegetables eleven times in a row. I guess the theory is that kids need to get accustomed to the idea that the veggie is going to be around for awhile before they become convinced to gobble it up.

The same theory applies to lead generation in real estate. You've got to be persistent when generating leads. People are not just going to gobble up what's on your plate the very first time you reach out to them.

To that end, use a lead generation follow-up program to reach out to prospects eleven times over a period of two or three weeks. You can create your own program or download one from the resource page on my website.

Given the cost of generating each individual lead, it seems foolish to let the lead slip through your fingers. That's why you need to be persistent and follow up regularly.

### Will You Flop Too?

Remember that Dick Fosbury's dedication and his unique way of getting over the high jump revolutionized track and field, but it took him three years to achieve great success and ultimately increase the height of his jump by nearly eighteen inches.

How many times do you think Fosbury ran down the field and attempted to launch his body into the air before he achieved success? I'm willing to bet that he was a lot more persistent and made a lot more attempts than you will need to make in order to obtain your next listing appointment.

## Double the Effort, Double the Earnings?

There is a dark side of consistency and dedication. It's when you work so hard and generate so many leads that you have spread yourself too thin; you have overcommitted.

I've done it before, and it wasn't pretty. I was once invited to a block party where each family was given two bags of semisweet chocolate chips and instructed to whip up something delicious to bring to the event.

Since I am not a super creative cook, I decided to use my two bags and follow the traditional chocolate chip cookie recipe—doubling it, of course.

I discovered quickly that if you do not have a baker's kitchen and bakery equipment, you may not be able to efficiently double the recipe.

I only realized that my mixer was too small to handle all of the batter when it was too late. I didn't realize until late in the process that I did not have enough cookie sheets to prepare so many cookies. I also didn't realize that I did not have the arm strength or the patience to scoop out one hundred beautiful cookies.

The whole idea sounded great when I got started. But in dedicating myself to a process that was too big for one person, I was foiled.

I made a huge mess. I had to use and reuse the cookie sheets, and the oven was on for hours. At the end of the whole project, I asked myself, "Was it all worth it?"

The cookies came out pretty well. But I also learned a lesson: sometimes in an effort to save time, you are actually cutting off your nose to spite your face. I thought that I might as well make ninety-six cookies since I was already making forty-eight. I didn't have the tools or the manpower to do a good job. I was lucky my cookies were even edible.

### Increasing Your Marketing Efforts

Sometimes when I try to double up on my marketing efforts or multitask to be more efficient, I seem to spread myself too thin. I do not end up putting my best efforts into my work—in the same way that my cookie experience kind of died a slow death.

There's a limit to the number of listings my team can handle, the number of short sales we can negotiate.

If we take on too many, then we are spreading ourselves too thin. We are not able to provide the level of service and dedication that our clients expect. We are not able to provide the kind of service that we want to provide. We show up, but we are scattered and overwhelmed.

Doubling up on the number of listings we take on does not always mean that we double the number of closings just as doubling the chocolate chip cookie recipe did not quite yield the experience I had hoped. It's about making the number of cookies that you can actually manage. Being successful at that . . . now that's dedication.

## How to Market to Your Sphere of Influence

Marketing is another big area of business where putting your nose to the grindstone really pays off. Advertising and lead generation are important aspects of building your business, and these activities must be completed day in and day out.

It's common to hear real estate agents discuss how they are spending their ad dollars. Some of the ways that agents spend advertising dollars include direct mail, blogging, Internet websites, social media, Craigslist, signs, promotional items, newsletters, gifts, sponsorships, and pay-per-click ads.

This is a pretty comprehensive list, but I am sure that many agents have a few other tricks and tools that also lead to great success. One item that is glaringly absent from the list in the previous paragraph is database management.

## Your Circle of Influence

Marketing to your sphere or circle of influence always proves to be a significant source of future business. It must be done. It must be done. It must be done thoroughly and regularly.

Like clockwork, you must manage your database and target and work your sphere. Top-producing agents have great success with two monthly mailers to the sphere and a minimum of one phone call per month. If your sphere members use the Internet, you can add the Internet to the mix or possibly substitute it for the mailers.

There are many customer relationship management (CRM) programs available for maintaining your data. Technology, particularly your smartphone, makes it easy for you to have access to all of the information about your clients not only when you are at your desk but also when you are out in the field. But no matter what tool you use to maintain your data, you must create a list of contacts.

In order to begin the process of regularly marketing to your sphere, you must create a list of all of the individuals in your sphere of influence. These are people that you know—that know your name and know that you are in the real estate business. These are people that will recognize you when you walk down the street or when you are at the supermarket or gas station.

If you have never created a database of your sphere of influence before, plan ahead. Creating this database will take at least two or three days of full-time work.

## Create or Refine Your Database

First, begin with your closed real estate transactions. It does not matter whether you have been in the business for one year or for ten. Add each and every individual that you have represented in a real estate transaction to your list.

Remember that if you have not communicated with these individuals recently, they may have moved. You will need to carefully verify all the contact information or send out a piece of test mail, and take note of which mail pieces are returned to sender.

Next, add all of the contacts from your cell phone and from your e-mail inbox. Now move on to your holiday card list, your school directories, your address book, and the stack of business cards piled on your desk or tacked to your bulletin board. Last, think about all of the professionals that you do business with every day: doctors, lawyers, dentists, educators, landscapers, and plumbers, among others. Add all of those folks to the list.

If all goes well, your list should include between one hundred and two hundred individuals.

Finally, you will need to verify their phone, e-mail, and mailing address. Unless you've had recent communication, you will need to confirm that each person's contact information is still valid. There are several online tools that can help you. And many Realtors® have access to additional resources, such as title company online systems and MLS data.

It doesn't hurt to review your database a few times a year. After all, you want your marketing materials to land at the right location, don't you? That's how your past clients and friends will know that are you not only a Realtor® today but also a professional real estate consultant for life.

> Loads of information about real estate lead conversion, time management, and short sale incentive programs among other topics can be found on the *Been There, Done That* resource page at www.melissazavala.com

# TRUST IN CHANGE
## The Principle of Adaptability

Policies change. People change. The real estate market changes. Many of us were searching properties in MLS books bigger than the Yellow Pages not so long ago. And now we can complete an entire transaction without even printing a single sheet of paper.

The interesting thing about change is that sometimes it happens and we barely even notice it. Or other times, the need for change is obvious, and if we don't embrace it, we may be rendered obsolete.

Over twenty years have elapsed since I first saw the movie *Grease*. As a young person, I loved that movie—the catchy tunes, the good-looking actors, the whole shebang. I must've watched it ten or twenty times when I was a kid. I even owned the album!

After seeing *Grease* again recently, I found that I still loved the catchy tunes. But what was even more notable to me this time around were the deliberate transformations made by the characters at the end of the movie.

You may recall that the main character, Sandy Olsson (played by Olivia Newton-John), is an Australian-born teenager that dresses and acts very conservatively. She is quaint, naive, and maybe a bit prudish.

Despite her attempts to gain the amorous attention of her high school crush, Danny Zuko (played by John Travolta), the "in" group of teenagers at school does not readily accept her. She just appears too conservative and seems so unlike the other students—a stick in the mud.

At the turning point in the movie, Sandy takes charge of her image and makes a transformation.

In the final scene, Sandy appears completely remade. She is wearing sexy black spandex pants, a snuggly fitted top, and high-heeled sandals. She has applied lots of makeup, and her hair is teased high on her head—not in the traditional, conservative style she wore for most of the movie.

Danny, her crush, who had equally changed himself from greasy street punk to clean-cut letterman athlete to win her love, accepts her, and they ride into the sunset—supposedly happily ever after.

It may be hard to believe, but this movie, and this last scene in particular, sends a really great message about the benefits of making a drastic transformation when necessary.

Sandy is forced to reinvent herself to get what she wants. She adapts (which takes her the entire school year to do) to her new lifestyle at her high school and in the United States. By making a transformation, she is able to achieve her goal, albeit perhaps a youthful and foolish one, of uniting with Danny Zuko.

You will probably also be called upon to make drastic alterations to your professional behaviors to win the love of an ever-changing real estate market.

In 2007, when the bottom began to fall out, naysayers felt that they did not want to work on distressed property sales because they were too much trouble.

Due to the significant increase in these challenging transactions, the everyday activities of a real estate professional were shifting in front of their eyes. So many agents rejected this market, in fact, that the National Association of Realtors® reported a 27 percent decline in membership during this time.

Being successful in real estate involves embracing change, not fighting it. While it may not mean wearing spandex pants like Sandy Olsson, it does often mean doing things that are slightly out of your comfort zone.

## *Seasoned Agents Can Adapt to Change*

The quality of being able to transition well comes easier to some people than to others. As the real estate market is continuously evolving, you must always be willing to adapt to the needs of the market—whatever they might be.

Here are three ways to more easily embrace changes as they occur:

**Change Tip No. 1: *Get educated.***

If your local real estate board is offering a class on something that seems to be on the horizon, you should attend. If you hear about a new topic (a new technology or popular way of doing business), there are plenty of free online webinars that can walk you through the process.

**Change Tip No. 2: *Watch online videos, and subscribe to newsletters.***

Once you have identified an area that you should embrace or where you need to refine your skills, use the Internet to become a master. Take advantage of the free short instructional videos on YouTube to learn something new. Or seek out and subscribe to online newsletters or RSS feeds offered by real estate and marketing experts. Using these tools can keep you up-to-date on whatever new topic comes your way.

**Change Tip No. 3:** *Listen to audiobooks.*

As a real estate professional, you probably spend lots of time in your car. Subscribe to podcasts or purchase audiobooks, and listen to brief excerpts as you drive around town. You'll be amazed at how satisfying it is to complete an entire instructional book or motivational tape about the latest way of doing business while not decreasing your time spent on other activities.

In order to succeed, real estate agents need to be willing to adapt and to grow. If you find yourself complaining about the market or some aspect of it, try to redirect your negative energy.

The time you spend complaining could be better spent refining your skills and learning more about the latest or newest ways of doing business.

## ADVICE FROM THE FRONT LINE

### *The Unique Flavors of a Real Estate Transaction*

Seasoned real estate agents know that no two sales transactions are ever the same. The unique flavors of each transaction are as specific as ingredients in a recipe.

In any real estate transaction, the situations that arise are specific to the property, to the negotiations, and to the parties involved. Yet our experience from one transaction to the next often gives us enough background and skill to adapt and solve new problems as they occur.

The unique flavors of each transaction are kind of like a featured recipe I once saw for a chocolate bacon cupcake. When I saw the recipe, I did a double take. "What the heck is this? What is it *gonna* taste like? Breakfast and dessert all in one?" I wondered.

I couldn't, for the life of me, imagine what that cupcake might taste like when I put it into my mouth (if I were brave enough to do that). I imagine that it would be something like the stick of chewing gum that Violet Beauregarde began chewing in *Charlie and the Chocolate Factory*—the gum that tasted like a three-course meal of tomato soup, roast beef, and blueberry pie.

It's the same way with short sales and with traditional real estate transactions—you just never know exactly what may happen because there are so many disparate factors.

## No Two Short Sales Are the Same

Just as I wouldn't know what to expect from the unique mix of flavors in that cupcake, I never know quite what to expect when working on a short sale.

It's not uncommon for me to receive calls from sellers who are considering listing their home as a short sale. They generally ask me the same questions about the length of the process, the impact on credit, and whether the bank will accept their particular hardship. Agents also reach out to me when they need assistance in adapting their hard skills to the distressed property market.

In the last several years, I have negotiated more short sales than I can count. Each one was different. With each successive negotiation, I was always surprised by the new and interesting ways that the "bacon" had mixed with the "chocolate." Would the transaction move quickly, or would the paperwork get lost between the fax machine and the bank's database?

What I can say is this: my experiences have taught me to be an expert strategist. I can anticipate what will probably occur and use leverage, contacts, and experience to obtain the best result possible for the client.

More importantly, if I need to, I can adapt my work style, my methods, and my negotiation strategies to get the short sale approved. However, I cannot guarantee with 100 percent accuracy what might happen, just as I am not quite sure about the flavor of that chocolate bacon cupcake.

## How Agents React When Faced with Challenge

Several years ago, I saw an article about how the works of William Shakespeare were actually authored by a Jewish woman. As a former teacher of English, I am particularly knowledgeable about Shakespeare and English literature. This new theory, however, was one that I had never heard before, and it caught me off guard.

Interestingly, I can relate my response to this particular curveball to the big change in our real estate market over the last several years.

All that seasoned real estate agents had been taught about how to sell real estate—how to go after expired listings, cancelled listings, and even for sale by owners—has changed quite a bit with the creation and continuous development of the Internet and social media platforms.

Also, all that we have been taught about pricing, negotiating terms, and working with clients is significantly different now in cities still plagued by distressed properties and **underwater borrowers**.

### Do You Make the Plants Wilt?

I once heard real estate coach Tom Ferry say something to the effect of "Everyone has an agent in their office who makes the plants wilt when they come in the door."

I'm sure you know that agent. It's Mr. Gloom or Ms. Doom. It's the agent who harkens back to the days of yore when property values were high, loans grew on trees, and buyers and sellers would walk in and hire you off of the street. They're the ones who cannot—or do not—learn, grow, and adapt. Instead, they develop a negative attitude, which makes the plants wilt.

Mr. Gloom and Ms. Doom are likely challenged by the changes to the market, the new technology, and all of the multitasking now required in order to have a competitive advantage.

These agents may not be accustomed to late nights, long dialogues, creative strategizing, and general hard work. Instead of embracing change, they have a negative reaction—possibly out of fear or because of the challenge often associated with learning something new.

I envision that Mr. Gloom and Ms. Doom feel kind of like I felt when I read that perhaps William Shakespeare's works were written by a woman. I felt stunned, surprised, and unsure of how to wrap my head around this new curveball. I felt a little bit uncomfortable that what I had learned (and taught others) might not be accurate.

Many agents probably feel that way about the market—stunned, surprised, and unsure. Here's the difference, though, and the take-away that I want you to catch.

When I finished reading the article, I picked myself up, got in the car, and went about my business—my real estate business. I made some calls. I did some paperwork. I attended to my clients. No plants wilted.

When life throws you a curve, just move out of the way of the ball, and keep moving. Only then will you arrive at your destination!

## Adapt or Go Out of Business

In 2012, Hostess, the maker of such iconic baked goods as Twinkies, Sno Balls, and Ding Dongs, requested permission from the bankruptcy court to cease operations. If you didn't turn on the television or listen to the radio that week, then you missed out on some interesting banter.

There were countless stories about people flocking to the shelves of every possible grocer across the nation so that they could purchase the very last Twinkies ever made.

What would the world do without these wonderful snack cakes? Would it be the end of an era? Would these tasty treats go away forever? And how would we survive if they did?

At that time, I bet dollars to Ding Dongs that we would see a newer and better Hostess in the coming weeks and months. And while Twinkies didn't return to the shelves for about eighteen months, they're back now. Lucky for us, we can live to eat them another day.

While I do not claim to know anything about the finances of the Hostess corporation prior to their bankruptcy filings, I can tell you one thing: Hostess wasn't known for its healthy fare.

In a society now consumed by thoughts of high-fiber flatbread and gluten-free pizzas, it's possible that Hostess should have considered embracing change. In order to continue to be successful, Hostess needed to be able to continually assess the market and adapt their products and marketing strategies accordingly.

## Transition with the Market

As a real estate agent, you also need to be able to adapt to the changing needs of the consumer. You must transition with the market. You need to identify the needs of home buyers and home sellers and address those needs before your services become obsolete.

Around 2007, agents suddenly went from selling homes at the blink of an eye to complaining about the economy, the Great Recession, and the real estate market. Agents who embraced the new normal (then short sales and foreclosures) continued to thrive despite the economic shift.

While the market never stops changing, some areas of the United States continue to have an influx of underwater homeowners and those living paycheck to paycheck who may desperately need to sell their homes today.

Other areas of the country are deluged with investor buyers yet challenged by low seller inventory. Whatever the consumer need may be, it is your responsibility to recognize it and address it in your prospecting and marketing activities.

It's tough to adapt to the changing needs of the marketplace. It's also tough to identify those needs and structure a plan to address them.

Are you going to continue to sell Twinkies, or are you going to make changes to what you do? The way I see it, you have two choices: adapt or get out of the business.

## *Know Your Market*

If you plan to stay in the real estate game (and I hope that you will), you need to regularly assess your knowledge of the market.

Here are some tips for identifying and adapting to the new normal—no matter what that might be.

### Tip No. 1: *Regularly analyze the market.*

It's a good idea to always keep an eye on the real estate market in your area of the country. Check out the inventory of available homes at each price point, and recognize whether you are in the midst of a seller's or a **buyer's market**. If it's a seller's market (a market consumed by low inventory), use strategies to obtain listings that you can sell quickly and for top dollar. If you are in the midst of a buyer's market, seek buyers, and find them good deals on available properties.

### Tip No. 2: *Keep tabs on the economy.*

Things going on in regard to economic news can send signals to you as to what you need to do in order to be successful. For example, if the unemployment rate is high, there may be an influx of home-owners that need to sell today. Also, when unemployment is high, it's best to locate investor or cash buyers since there will be significantly fewer buyers able to qualify for a mortgage.

**Tip No. 3:** *Understand available mortgage programs.*

The mortgage market often gives us clues as to how we need to change our business model. When lending guidelines are very tight or if Fannie Mae and Freddie Mac are purchasing fewer homes on the secondary market, it is going to be more difficult to put certain buyers into homes—those that have a small down payment. Seek out cash buyers or those with larger down payments in order to maximize what some may perceive as an unfortunate situation.

If you are looking to see success in real estate, then you need to recognize that a large part of your success is based on how well you make transitions. The best agents in the business constantly evaluate the market and the economy and shift gears when necessary. I'm not sure whether they eat Twinkies or gluten-free pizza, but chances are they're pretty flexible when it comes to all things real estate.

## ADVANCING TO NEW TERRAIN

### *Understand Your Value in the Marketplace*

The market is always changing. New agents come; old agents go. The financial picture shifts. Something different and new is always just around the corner.

Are you prepared? Are you happy with what you have achieved so far in your career? What ideas and strategies have worked well? What was a big waste of time and money? What do you need to be doing today to change with the times?

In order to know where to adapt, you need to start by identifying where you are right now. To do this, you must be acutely aware of your competition. If you spend a little bit of time looking at your competition and analyzing how and what they are doing, this will help you to devise your own plans for increased success.

I used to think that a careful market analysis was a fruitless exercise and a waste of time. But then I changed my mind.

In late 2007, I decided that I wanted to take my little short sale negotiation niche to the next level. I wanted to combine my great skills and successes in that area with my former talents as a high school and college English teacher. My plan was to share my passion for distressed property sales through workshops and seminars.

I called a semiretired cousin of mine who provided business consulting services. Earlier in his career, he was a marketing giant and created huge businesses and large streams of income. Semiretired, he devoted several hours that year to charity work—dealing with me.

What we did was to generate a formal written business plan.

I thought I understood my goals and plans, but after I spent ten or twenty hours developing the plan and putting my thoughts into writing, I found that I had a much better sense of what I wanted to do and how I was going to do it.

Putting my own thoughts on paper allowed me to clarify the direction I wanted to take in my career; it also helped me to understand my value in the marketplace.

## *Identify Your Competitive Advantage*

In order to develop a clear idea of what you plan to achieve next in your business, start by examining your competition. You will want to understand what they offer, what you offer, and how your services provide unique value—just as I did when I analyzed my role as a short sale expert.

Follow these instructions to identify your competitive advantage.

1. Identify three competitors.

2. On scratch paper or on your computer, make a chart with four columns. At the top of column 1, write your name. Then at the

top of each of the other columns, write the names of three of your competitors.

3.  In the rows below your name, write every reason that a person might hire you.

4.  What are the benefits of each competitor? List those benefits in the rows below each of your competitors. To help you get started, you may want to consider why a buyer or seller might hire each competitor—instead of you—to aid in a real estate transaction.

5.  When you're done listing all the benefits, cross off all of the common or duplicate ones. If all individuals provide great customer service, for example, then cross it off the list.

What remains in your column is a list of benefits that can become your competitive advantage. Your advantage is why people will hire you instead of your competitors. It's what you should be advertising and touting in all of your marketing materials or wherever you have the opportunity to sell your services.

Once you analyze and evaluate your competitors, you may identify areas where you need to adapt and change in order to offer a better range of services. Being acutely aware of where you stand in the changing marketplace will help you to both sell your services and also convey the unique benefits you provide.

## *The Internet Is the Great Equalizer*

In 2011, the Texas Rangers headed to the World Series. It may be old news now, but did you know that getting to the Series was their biggest victory in the franchise's fifty-year history? Interestingly, the team's budget was only a small percentage of the budget of their rival, the Giants.

Even though my favorite team, the Red Sox, didn't make it to the Series that year, I enjoyed watching. I love it when underdogs make it to the top. I loved watching Butler University at the NCAA tournament in 2010. Their performance, as another underdog, was truly amazing.

One really great benefit of technology is that it evens the playing field for the little people—the underdogs.

Now real estate agents can directly compete with large conglomerates for placement on page 1 of Google or other search engines. And frequently, the underdog wins! You just have to be willing to learn how to master the Internet in order to make that happen.

When I was a kid, we got our information from the television or the newspaper. We listened to music on local radio stations and purchased albums at the record store. There were fewer ways for underdogs to be competitive—unless you had big bucks (but then you wouldn't be an underdog, would you?).

Now through the Internet, we can create niches to convey our uniqueness, target our specialty market, and demonstrate results just as favorable as the big guys. We can use YouTube, Twitter, Facebook, and other social media sites to create the followings previously only available if you were a member of a rock star fan club.

I'm constantly amazed by how much the Internet and social media have leveled the virtual playing field.

When real estate agents get educated about the Internet and use it successfully, even the smallest businesses—even a single agent working alone—can compete with the large IDX sites and show up at the top of the search results. That's the kind of change that can make any agent successful.

## Good Content Levels the Playing Field

Whether it's using social media, blogging, or making videos, it's a new world out there. It's no longer enough just to send out mailers and attend a few networking events. You have to understand the value of online content to your success.

With the Internet as the great equalizer, quality content is what can help you get to the top. You already know that 90 percent of home buyers and home sellers begin their search on the Internet, so that's where you need to be—creating content that lands on page 1 of Google or other search engines.

Here are some tips to consider when incorporating content creation into your marketing calendar:

### Content Creation Tip No. 1: *Plan ahead.*

Blogging requires planning. When I write a blog post, I think about what I am trying to communicate and what supporting material or reference links I may require.

Content is king, and spending the time to check facts and to dot your i's and cross your t's is important. The goal is to make every post helpful, substantial, and good. To achieve that, you must have a plan. You cannot just regurgitate information and throw it out there at the eleventh hour.

Good content builds trust. People will see you as a trustworthy expert, and this will enhance your professional image.

### Content Creation Tip No. 2: *Identify and know your audience.*

Knowing who you are writing to and for is key. If you are a novice blogger or an inconsistent blogger, you need to do some research and clearly identify your audience. Audience is a huge factor that needs to be considered before writing each and every post.

Wherever I have an online column, I always consider the audience. If the audience on a particular website is real estate agents, then I think about what these readers are seeking from the website.

Do they want short sale training? Do they want lead generation tips? Or if the audience is home buyers or home sellers, what kinds of information are they looking for?

Understanding the unique concerns and issues of each audience helps me provide information that readers will find valuable.

### Content Creation Tip No. 3: *Create a writing schedule.*

After you have identified your audience, you must establish a writing schedule. In online industry terms, this is called an editorial calendar.

What are you going to write about, and how often are you going to post? For me, I devote one day each week to my writing, and then I schedule the articles or posts to syndicate at specific times during the week. For others, they allocate a little bit of time each day to writing and posting.

Whether you decide to write once a week or once a day, create an editorial calendar and stick to it.

### Content Creation Tip No. 4: *Be original.*

If you write several blog posts per week, they must be filled with good content. Good original content—not something that you copied from someone else's site and not a quick link to an article that you read in the *Wall Street Journal.* A high-quality original piece of writing is what will attract attention and convert.

### Content Creation Tip No. 5: *Share the spotlight.*

It's helpful to do a lot of linking to other people's writing in your posts. I do this in order to cite a source or to provide additional information of value. My thought is that if I provide something of value for free, I am sure to generate a stronger online following.

It's true! I have generated a following. I have thousands of subscribers to my weekly short sale newsletter, and as I mentioned earlier, I have had several home sellers call me and say, "Please come list my house." No interview was necessary. This is the power of consistent and high-quality content.

Remember that content is king, and you do not want to be seen as the court jester! Do your homework, plan a bit, and share your original point of view. You'll build trust and develop a larger client base, all of whom will continue to follow you in an ever-changing real estate market.

## Minor Changes Can Make You Exceptional

Film director Jean-Luc Godard once said, "It's not where you take things from—it's where you take them to." What he meant by this is that nothing is truly original. Instead, it is your representation or adaptation of the materials of others that makes it your own.

Consider *The Last Supper* as an example. How many times have you seen this scene depicted in a museum? Probably much more than just once. But it is each artist's unique interpretation of this famous scene that shows their style, shares their feelings, and sends a unique message to the viewer.

When it comes to sending unique messages to home buyers and home sellers, you don't need to be truly original in the real estate services you provide or the marketing materials that you create. You can change and adapt a certain way of doing things and make it your own.

### Make Something Unoriginal Your Own

Musicians are constantly covering the songs of other musicians. Sid Vicious covered Sinatra's "My Way," and Ike and Tina Turner covered "Proud Mary," which was an original of Creedence Clearwater Revival. Each of these singers reinvented the song and presented it in their own way.

As businesspeople, we continuously need to be reinventing ourselves and refreshing our image, our marketing techniques, and our product in order to address the changing needs of the consumer.

These famous covers show us that we don't need to reinvent the wheel. We can actually take something unoriginal that's already there—something that's right in front of our eyes—and make it our own.

The goal is to be exceptional, and this can be accomplished not only by leaps and bounds, but also in the small things you do every day.

## Tips for Personalized Customer Service

Here are three small changes that you can make to set your business apart from the rest:

### Customer Service Tip No. 1: *Answer the phone.*

Have you ever been involved in a long exchange via e-mail? People often defer to e-mail and text messages when a simple phone call will address questions and alleviate concerns in a much shorter period of time. Not to mention, in a phone call, you can actually sell your services or your product through tone and voice quality.

A phone call, while increasingly an obsolete method of communication, often sets your customer service skills apart from the rest.

### Customer Service Tip No. 2: *Make physical contact.*

(Sounds dirty, doesn't it?) All joking aside, if you've ever shopped at Nordstrom, then you know that each and every item purchased at the store is neatly wrapped in a shopping bag, which is handed to you by an employee that walks around the counter and with whom you have direct contact. No item is passed over a counter or placed in a bag on a winding turnstile for you to pick up as you head out the door.

This simple technique sends the message that the customer is very important and special. Think about it . . . how easy is it to walk over and give somebody a bag? Consider what you can do to send that same kind of message.

**Customer Service Tip No. 3: *Respond to everyone daily.***

Almost everywhere I go and everyone that I have contact with rants about some unreturned phone call or an individual that appears to have gone AWOL. In fact, I may actually still be waiting for that return phone call from the doctor's office.

You can set yourself apart by responding to all of your phone messages and e-mails every day—instead of ignoring them or leaving them for tomorrow. In a world where this is increasingly uncommon, people like to know that they've been heard.

Getting face-to-face with consumers and adding your personal touch are not so difficult, and they can make a big difference. Your customers feel special because you have paid attention to them instead of sending a brief text or shooting off an e-mail.

Even if you cannot sing half as well as Sid Vicious or Ike Turner and even if your product isn't as high-end as the jewelry sold at Nordstrom, these simple changes to your daily activities can make your business exceptional.

---

Tips and tools relating to the information provided in this chapter can be found on the *Been There, Done That* resource page at www.melissazavala.com

---

# HAVE A HEART
## The Principle of Empathy

The words "real estate professional" are often loosely used to describe any salesperson or broker that works in the field of real estate. Yet true "real estate professionals" are not a dime a dozen. They care for clients, protect them from harm, and conduct their business in an ethical manner.

Sometimes people interpret the word "professional" to mean unfeeling, objective, and borderline ruthless. Professionalism is important, and managing the expression of a client's emotions during a sales transaction is an often-overlooked aspect of what it means to be a real estate professional.

Losing a home or selling a home can be a very emotional experience. That's why it's important to identify your clients' needs and understand their feelings and points of view.

You can be the best paper pusher in the world, but you'd be nowhere if you were not sensitive to the emotional needs of the people you work with.

The agents who are best at what they do are those who are entirely genuine, those who really want to help their clients. These agents earn a good living in real estate because they are not so exceedingly focused on the next commission check. They do not let the pursuit of money get in the way of acting as a responsible fiduciary on behalf of their clients.

They help their clients select the best buyer or find the most suitable home, even if their clients' choices will not net the agent top dollar.

When you genuinely care about the well-being of your clients, people take note. A healthy balance of compassion and business acumen will lead to increased closings and lifelong referrals.

## A Match Not Made in Heaven

Several years ago, I received a referral from an agent in Los Angeles. This agent and I were in the same referral network, and the prospective sellers that she referred were two elderly sisters who wanted to sell their condominium as a short sale.

I was excited about the prospect of a new listing. With my track record of success in short sales, I thought that this listing would be easy, that it would barely take any of my time.

Boy, was I wrong! While these women were as sweet as can be, we were not a good emotional match. I recognized that fact early in the process but did not have the heart to part ways.

You see, I'm all business. While I am understanding and sensitive to the fact that sellers are losing their home, I am also objective.

I see myself as having been hired to do a job. My job is to process the short sale; find a ready, willing, and able buyer; and assure that the sellers have as stress-free a transaction as humanly possible.

My job is not, however, to be a psychologist.

These sisters had huge emotional needs that took hours upon hours to fulfill. Each telephone conversation or meeting was at least two hours long, and we could have multiple meetings in one week. They would ask many, many questions about the short sale process, and I would often have to explain the same thing several times in multiple ways.

Unfortunately, for a number of reasons beyond my control, the short sale was not an easy one. And because of this, the sellers became more anxious, wanted more meetings, and relied on me for hours each week to listen to their concerns and answer their questions.

While the transaction is now long closed and the sellers have been a great source of referrals, this lovely pair of sisters is a good reminder that it helps to have a heart.

While I am grateful for all of the subsequent referrals, being an emotional crutch for someone in trouble (selling in short sale or perhaps after the death of a loved one) is demanding. You have to be up for the task.

## Tips for Connecting with Your Clients

Clearly, it's important to be empathetic, and you have to genuinely want to help the people that have hired you. But it's not just the desire to help that's important.

You must demonstrate the ability to step into the shoes of another person, aiming to understand their perspectives and feelings and to use that understanding to guide your actions.

It's different from sympathy, kindness, or pity. Showing empathy means discovering your client's feelings and using those feelings in order complete the sale with their best interests at heart.

Here are three ways to show empathy for your clients:

**Empathy Tip No. 1:** *Listen, listen, and listen.*

Being a good listener means that there is no texting, e-mailing, or answering the phone when you are meeting with a client.

When your clients see that you are fully focused on their needs, then the transaction will move along swimmingly.

**Empathy Tip No. 2: *Ask questions.***

In order to understand the situation at hand, ask open-ended questions about your client's needs. The more you can learn about your clients and their thoughts at the beginning of the transaction, the easier it will be to work toward a successful outcome.

When people feel heard and emotionally understood, they often relax, open up, and feel supported. Asking people how they truly feel is one of the best ways to express empathy for your clients.

**Empathy Tip No. 3: *Don't bite off more than you can chew.***

If you are not going be able to complete the transaction on good terms and you already recognize that from the time of the listing appointment, you probably should refer the listing to somebody else. Don't agree to do something unless you are confident that you will be successful on a financial and an emotional level.

Never take a listing unless you are confident that you can stay on good terms with the clients through closing.

Having a good heart-to-heart with your clients at the beginning of the transaction will assure that you understand their needs. You don't have to agree with them or fully understand them to be able to empathize.

You don't even need to be able to relate to what they are experiencing specifically (although that can help). You just need to be present, connect with them where they are, and acknowledge what they're experiencing.

At the same time, it is also important that they understand your feelings and perspectives and that they acknowledge what you're experiencing too.

Discussing expectations puts everyone on an even playing field as you move forward with the real estate transaction, whether it's a short sale or a traditional one.

When working on your real estate transaction, keep it real and manage emotions and expectations while, at the same time, aiming to understand feelings and perspectives.

Remember that you must have a heart. Being professional or "all business" does not mean being unfeeling.

---

## ADVICE FROM THE FRONT LINE

### *Which Is Better: Short Sale or Foreclosure?*

Home sellers frequently ask about the benefits of selling their home as a short sale as opposed to intentionally letting it go to foreclosure. Top agents are always ready to provide honest answers to those questions. During what can be a very traumatic time, being a solid source of information can be calming.

Anyone facing foreclosure should always consult with a qualified attorney or accountant, and real estate professionals should never advise beyond the scope of their expertise.

Despite the fact that some clients may ask questions beyond the agent's scope, savvy distressed property experts must be able to answer the most common questions asked by prospective short sale sellers.

The following list reviews the most common seller concerns:

**Seller Question No. 1:** *What will happen to my credit score?*

*Answer*: In a foreclosure, your credit score (**FICO score**) may be lowered more than 250 points. Typically, this will impact your credit for a period of five years.

In a short sale, late payments or lack of a payment on your mortgage will show up on your credit report.

Once the short sale is complete, your mortgage company will report your mortgage as "paid as agreed," "settled," or "paid as negotiated."

The short sale closing can lower the credit score as little as twenty-five points, and the impact on the credit score may be as brief as one or two years. The best source of further information on this matter would be a local loan officer since loan officers see credit scores and credit reports as part of their daily activities.

**Seller Question No. 2: *Will the lender pursue a deficiency judgment?***

*Answer:* In a foreclosure, the bank may have the right to pursue a deficiency judgment.

In a short sale, it is possible to convince the lender to give up the right to pursue the deficiency judgment.

In certain states, there are anti-deficiency statutes that prohibit the lender from pursuing a deficiency. The United States Treasury also has some programs where lenders are not permitted to pursue deficiency.

If you are participating in a short sale, the mortgage lender will provide a short sale approval letter. This letter usually specifies whether the lender plans to pursue deficiency.

**Seller Question No. 3: *How will a short sale or a foreclosure impact my future ability to borrow?***

*Answer:* In a foreclosure, borrowers may have to disclose on a loan application whether they have a property that has been foreclosed on within the last seven years.

On the other hand, sellers that participate in a short sale may have the opportunity to purchase in as little as two years. For an extremely limited number of short sale sellers, there are even opportunities to purchase again right away.

Local lenders and loan officers can best advise you as to whether you would qualify for one of these programs.

Part of expressing empathy means being able to educate clients and assist them in making more informed decisions. That's why you need to know the answers or at least know where to get those answers.

Each distressed borrower's situation is unique, and it's always important to advise clients and prospective clients with their best interests—not your best interests—at heart.

## The Best Way to Get Short Sales Approved

I'm not going to try and sell you on any newly invented device that purports to help you get your short sales approved. I also have not invented a software platform or website that will help you earn top commission while not having to make a single phone call to the bank.

Like many agents, you are probably hoping for convenience and ease, but I cannot offer that.

I am going to share the best way to get your short sales approved. It's not rocket science, so I think you can start using it right away, even if you don't have an advanced scientific degree.

A long time ago, I happened upon this method that gets short sales approved. Truth be told, I already knew the method. But I was reminded of it again as a result of a conversation with an out-of-area agent.

An agent from another state called my office and said that she was working with one of the major lending institutions on a short sale. The bank had presented a counteroffer that was about $30,000 higher than her buyer's offer.

This agent wanted to convince the bank that her buyer was a good buyer. Also, while the property may have been worth a few grand more, she wanted to move ahead with this buyer who would not increase the purchase price. She wanted me to advise her on how to convince the bank to accept her buyer's offer.

"What have you done so far?" I asked.

"Well," she said. "To tell you the truth, I haven't done much. I sent an e-mail to the negotiator to let her know that the buyer didn't want to move forward at the bank's price, and the negotiator said that she was closing the file. I've been really busy because I am in the midst of getting ready for a trip with my family."

Okay . . . so are you ready for the secret? Are you ready to hear the way short sales get approved?

Here it is: *You need to care.*

### You Need to Care

You need to care so hard that it keeps you up at night and wakes you up in the morning. You need to know off the top of your head which of your properties may be going to foreclosure this week, and you need to be prepared to make some calls early in the morning—maybe even in your pajamas.

You need to treat each and every client's home as if it were your own. You need to speak to each and every negotiator and bank employee as if "yes" is the only option because you are charged with what was once the biggest asset of your client's portfolio.

You can fax or e-mail paperwork until your poor little fingers are tired of pushing buttons. But if you are just going through the motions day in and day out, then you may not be seeing the short sale approval letters flying into your inbox.

Even if you are busy preparing for a family trip, the way to be successful is to be passionate and to care. Put some sugar on top and you have a recipe for success.

By the way, caring brings you success—not just in short sales, but in just about everything that you do. Of course, a little bit of skill doesn't hurt either.

## People Buy with Emotion, Not Logic

It's not uncommon for agents and sellers to become very emotional during the purchase or sale of a home, particularly in a short sale situation due to the added stress of the hardship and the dealings with the lender.

That being said, the more objective that agents (and sellers and buyers) can be, the higher the likelihood of success in the transaction.

Zig Ziglar once said, "People usually buy on emotion and they justify it with logic." And while Ziglar's theory may apply if you are trying to convince your spouse that you must have a new red Corvette, the short sale transaction will go a lot more smoothly if you can sit back and tap into the practical components only.

When working on short sales, I often hear comments from sellers and other agents such as "Tell the bank that I do not have the money" or "Tell the bank that they are forcing my client into foreclosure."

The thing about short sale processing is that even though those comments are true, they will do absolutely nothing to elicit a quick and efficient short sale approval letter.

I figured out a long time ago that the bank is not a thinking, feeling being. It is a business—and a very large one that is looking at its books, practices, and procedures when making decisions. It's all about debt settlement; it's not about you.

## Banks Are Like Puppies

The best way that it can be explained is like this: If you or someone you know has a new puppy, you may say or hear comments such as "My puppy is sad" or "My puppy is lonely." However, as you probably already realize, this is not the case. What happens is that folks project human feelings and traits onto their pets (also called anthropomorphizing).

I'm not saying that banks are animals, but if you project emotions on the bank in an attempt to negotiate terms, you will soon realize that this negotiation style will not lead to short sale success.

## Best Practices for Obtaining Short Sale Approval

One of the best ways to elicit short sale success is to provide the bank with the short sale documentation that they want. And if it is not enough to help the lender make a decision about approving a short sale, then you need to strategize.

Consider any other paperwork or documentation you could provide that will convince the lender to review and approve your short sale, while adhering to bank procedures and maintaining objectivity.

Once in a blue moon, you may have a short sale processor or a vice president that can override decisions and use a little bit of subjectivity. Sadly, however, this doesn't happen often enough.

Therefore, the best way to arrive at short sale success is to retrain your brain to remember that the bank doesn't have feelings. Banks are like puppy dogs, but probably not quite as cute.

## *Walk a Mile in the Lender's Shoes*

You may think that I have a shoe fetish. I've already told you about the intense order and detail of my grandmother's closet, particularly the fact that her shoes were organized by color.

Yes, like many women, I have a thing for shoes. I confess.

So in honor of shoes, I am going to reach into my vast knowledge about them and share a well-known proverb "Before you criticize a man, walk a mile in his shoes."

That is, do not criticize someone until you have actually been in his or her position, doing things as he or she does them.

Never has this proverb hit home for me more than in the last few years.

Over the last several years, I have negotiated over 1,500 short sale transactions. I have also read countless articles attacking banks and mortgage lenders for being inept, irresponsible, unprofessional, and disorganized.

Just like everyone else working short sales, I have been yelled at, bullied, and even disconnected. Yet I have somehow realized that it is not about me.

It is about understanding the overwhelming nature of the short sale from the point of view of the mortgage lender.

Here's what you need to think about when you are frustrated with the short sale lenders:

- You may sometimes have difficulty hiring one or two employees who are well qualified. The bank needs to hire hundreds of them.
- You may sometimes have difficulty with your office telephone system and its thirty extensions. The bank must have a telephone system one thousand times more sophisticated than your own.
- Your staff sometimes has difficulty managing thirty or forty files. Individual negotiators at some banks have over four hundred files.

Once you can understand the bank's position, you can successfully strategize to get the job done for your client.

I'm not saying that you need to pity the short sale lender. Remember that empathy means understanding feelings and perspective and then using that perspective to guide your actions.

That is, it's more likely that you will control the outcome once you walk in the lender's shoes.

Yes, I have learned to walk a mile in the mortgage lender's shoes. And it doesn't matter to me whether they are made by Manolo Blahnik or Nike.

## ADVANCING TO NEW TERRAIN

### *Free Food Replaces Good Service*

There are some businesses that offer free food as a way to get people in the door. If you think about it, what is the purpose of these free goodies? Are they offered as a replacement for great customer service, or are they offered in order to get prospects in the door that can later be converted into buyers?

Several years ago when we expanded our office, we needed to purchase an additional sofa for the lobby area.

I knew what I wanted and where I needed to go. This was nothing high-end. I assure you. I wanted to purchase a specific leather sofa from one of those discount furniture stores, a store that offers you popcorn and free cookies when you walk in the door.

So one Sunday, my husband and I took the twenty-minute drive to the furniture store. We walked in at around 2:45 p.m. We saw loads of sales people. We found the sofa and we were ready to purchase—all in about two minutes.

Suddenly, there was not a salesperson in sight. Isn't that how it usually goes?

My husband made the following suggestion so that we didn't have to do laps around the store in order to locate a salesperson: "Why not sit right here on the sofa and see how long it'll take for someone to approach us and ask if we need help?"

We weren't in a big hurry, and I kind of liked the idea of this interesting customer service experiment. So we sat . . . and sat . . . and sat.

Twelve minutes later, a woman approached us to see if she could help us. When I told her that I wanted to purchase the sofa, she became very excited because this was going to be her first sale of the day. "Really? I'm not surprised that she hasn't made any sales yet today." I thought.

It took over an hour to complete the transaction, which was riddled with poor service and misinformation.

Simply put, the entire experience was not that satisfying. What I saved by shopping at a discount furniture store, I spent in headaches and lost time. However, we were very fortunate because we received free popcorn and cookies.

After that day, I began to think about what kind of customer service clients expect.

What kind of service do clients deserve? I bought the furniture at a discount store. Does this mean I should receive a discounted level of service? If I offer my own clients free popcorn and cookies, does it mean that I do not have to provide a high level of service?

In North San Diego County, we have home prices ranging from $100,000 all the way up to millions of dollars. It doesn't matter whether I am taking a $100,000 listing or writing a 2 million dollar offer. I provide figurative popcorn and cookies to all my clients, and I never make them wait.

Each buyer or seller who walks in the door receives the same level of service; it's a good one—and they even get to sit on the couch!

## *Professionalism in Real Estate and Beyond*

You could probably spend more than a year of your life reading articles about civility and professionalism in real estate. I've seen posts by agents that complain about their colleagues not returning phone calls or being too abrasive.

I've also seen many a troll create discord in a seemingly innocuous online conversation. People often complain about comments from braggers or those who sell their own services and self-promote on someone else's blog.

Seth Godin said, "Anonymity is the enemy of civility."

What he meant in this quote is that when we are able to remain anonymous and when we are not acquainted with the individual with whom we are having dealings (or when we do not have to provide our own name and be accountable), then it is easier to act in a way that is less than civil and more unfeeling.

One of my biggest pet peeves is when a person in the express line at the supermarket pays with a check. It drives me bananas.

Usually, the individual who is writing the check does not pull out his or her checkbook until after the cashier has completed ringing up the order. Perhaps this individual does not even have a pen handy.

This makes me absolutely crazy. My theory is that an express line is created for individuals who have only a few items and it is designed so that people can get out quickly. When someone leisurely goes about writing a check, it takes away from the original intention of the express line.

Considering Godin's theory of anonymity, I wonder . . . if I was acquainted with the individual who was writing the check, would I be more tolerant? If this was an old friend or a colleague, would I even be angry or impatient? Or is this person's anonymity (the fact that I do not know them personally) what causes the decrease in my sensitivity?

For me, the anonymity is gone when you have professional interactions with others on the Internet. When I comment on a blog post, my photo and my name are connected with my comment.

So it is crucial that I am civil, professional and polite—even when I disagree. Anything I say could come back to haunt me, and people will know it's me because of my name and photo out there for the world to see.

If we all knew one another and were on a first-name basis, would the world generally be more civil? Would the issues that other bloggers are complaining about essentially be eradicated? Would the agent who does not return your phone call actually return your call because he knows you?

I'm not trying to preach peace and love (although that wouldn't be too bad). I'm just trying to point out that I agree with Godin when he said, "Anonymity is the enemy of civility."

If we all kept that in mind and treated everybody we met as a prospective client or someone we already knew, it might increase our closings and improve upon the way we do business.

## Gratitude Helps Cement Relationships

Everyone laments the sorry state of sales agents—that they do not return phone calls or even answer the telephone.

But it's probably also a good idea for real estate professionals to use the magic words "thank you." Don't you remember teaching your kids to always say "please" and "thank you"?

When I was a child, I remember that when my grandparents came over to visit, my grandfather would frequently jingle the change in his pockets, and my brother and I would somehow end up with a 10 dollar or 20 dollar bill.

We were thrilled, of course. More money for candy or toys. Our mother would require that we telephone the grandparents shortly after the visit in order to thank them for the gift.

Emily Post said, "It's never wrong to send a written thank-you, and people always appreciate getting 'thanks' in writing. Why? Handwritten notes are warmer and more special than other forms of thank-yous."

A thank-you note, a personal note, or a call is such a warm touch. It shows that you care. You can really impress someone with your good manners and your caring attitude, so why not take advantage of this easy opportunity to impress others by saying thanks or writing a thank-you note?

I personally receive more e-mails than I can count from other agents throughout the country who are soliciting advice on some real estate-related issue.

All of these e-mails have two things in common: (1) I answer them in great detail, and (2) very few senders say "thank you."

While Emily Post recommends thank-you notes for weddings and bar mitzvahs, she really doesn't mention what to do when Realtors® help one another.

However, if you are soliciting the advice of someone you have never met before and asking that person to take time out of his or her busy schedule to advise you on how to work through your job-related challenge, I'd say that a quick e-mail of gratitude might be in order.

Saying thanks shows that you have a heart and that you acknowledge and appreciate the other individual's time, effort, or dedication.

Gratitude, compassion, and understanding when working with your affiliates and when in communication with both buyers and sellers can go a long way toward success in real estate and beyond.

---

You can access videos and charts on short sales versus fore-closures on the *Been There, Done That* resource page at www.melissazavala.com

# LEND AN EAR
## The Principle of Attention

A key to successfully selling any product, service, or idea is to ask questions and then carefully and quietly pay attention to the answers. Many of us try too hard to convince people to buy instead of discovering what our future client really wants, needs, or desires from us.

Admittedly, sometimes it is more difficult to close your mouth than to keep it open. In real estate, it's not just about listening to your clients. There are other factions from which we can learn: our local affiliates and associated professionals, including mortgage lenders, loan officers, and title representatives.

Being able to take information in, synthesize it, and then ask good questions is crucial to success in real estate.

Year after year, when I was working with bank employees on short sales and it was holiday season, I could usually tell you what each one of those individuals wanted for Christmas.

I remember one man telling me that he wouldn't be at his office the next day because he had tickets to some big concert. Another was taking a weeklong trip to Florida. And another loved to make salsa from peppers and fresh vegetables that he purchased at the local farmer's market.

These were small details, but important ones. These were the details that got my short sales approved fast.

It wasn't always about the documentation, the purchase price, or even the settlement statement. Instead, it was often about being a good listener, connecting with the employees and leveraging those connections in order to solidify a relationship and often a closing.

In addition to learning about the bank employees' personal lives, it was also important to listen and learn about all aspects of the short sale process at each particular lending institution.

When an employee glossed over a rule or guideline, I would continuously press for more information.

I'd ask for every detail that the bank employee would divulge. I would note the responses and take time to synthesize the information provided.

Any detail I could obtain might later assist me in best representing my clients and getting that short sale or future short sales through the system as quickly and efficiently as possible.

## Three Reasons to Listen Carefully

Listening helps, and sometimes it is not easy to keep quiet. There are many benefits to asking questions and listening to the responses.

Listening can help you not only in solving problems but also in seeing another person's position. When you focus on paying attention, you develop deeper understanding, improve relationships, and are more successful.

Here are three reasons to listen carefully.

### Reason to Listen No. 1: *To cement relationships*

When you are a good listener and you actually hear and synthesize the things that you are told, including likes and dislikes and other small details about those who you listen to, you will be seen as someone who cares. That caring will help to cement business and personal relationships.

### Reason to Listen No. 2: *To increase efficiency when representing buyers*

If you listen to your buyers' needs—really listen—then you can better identify homes that they will like. As a result, you put them in homes more quickly and close deals more efficiently.

### Reason to Listen No. 3: *To work more effectively with affiliates*

You can better understand the entire real estate process—not just your part of it—when you take time to listen to what is required by lenders, settlement officers, and title insurance companies.

Once you have a good grip on their processes, you can close transactions with increased skill because you prepared paperwork or strategized based on the information you received.

Being a good listener means keeping your mouth closed. You've heard the saying "Less is more," right? Well, that applies to selling real estate as well. Listening means opening your ears and your mind and closing your mouth. It means that you need to shut up in order to sell.

## ADVICE FROM THE FRONT LINE

## *Don't You Dare Take the Listing Until . . .*

Even though more listings sounds like a great way to earn more money, asking some preliminary questions (and really listening to the answers) can go a long way toward securing a short sale listing that will actually make it all the way to the closing table.

When a client calls you to set a listing appointment or a consultation to discuss the possible short sale of his or her home, make sure to "prequalify" or "interview" that client on the telephone when setting up the appointment.

Ask questions to find out about the number of mortgage liens, whether the property taxes are current, whether any homeowner's association dues (if applicable) are current, and whether the borrower is still making the mortgage payments.

Then if you have not already done so, order a preliminary title report or a property profile from a title insurance company to verify the accuracy of the information that you obtained from the borrower via telephone.

Next, tell the borrower that in order for a mortgage lender to process a short sale, certain personal documents will need to be submitted.

Whether the sellers list the property at the appointment or whether the appointment is merely a consultation, it would be best if the borrower pulled together these documents for the meeting.

Tell the seller that the required documents include two months' pay stubs for all borrowers, two months' bank statements for all borrowers, two years' tax returns, and mortgage statements for all loans.

When the borrower is ready, set your appointment to go to the property to meet your prospective clients!

## Look for Clues to Assess Seller Motivation

Before taking a short sale listing, it's important to assess seller motivation. A motivated seller is an important component of the short sale process.

Listing agents need to be like Sherlock Holmes and look for clues—clues that the seller is going to be helpful and motivated throughout the listing period.

- Has the seller gathered the required documents for the appointment?
- Will the seller permit property showings at convenient times?

- Is the seller going to be forthcoming with the short sale lender?
- Does the seller have an exit strategy?
- Did the seller wait until one week before foreclosure to contact you?

Based on your observations, you can get a good idea about how helpful the seller will be during the short sale process. These observations will also help you determine the likelihood of a successful closing.

A seller without an exit strategy, for example, will be tough to get out of the home prior to closing. A listing taken one week prior to the auction date may end as a foreclosure.

Processing a short sale (from listing to closing) is not easy job. It takes a team, and your sellers need to be part of the team!

When you listen and assess verbal and nonverbal cues and adjust your position accordingly, you'll have a much clearer idea about whether there is a closing in your future.

## Can You Get My Short Sale Approved Fast?

Agents that want to list short sales need to be well prepared for the listing appointment. Savvy sellers that are seeking to hire a short sale agent will have done their research, and they will have many questions.

I frequently get phone calls from agents and short sale sellers who ask me how long it will take to get their short sale approved.

Short sales are very unique (like the flavors of a chocolate bacon cupcake), and the answers to any questions about a short sale often differ from short sale lender to short sale lender.

Some banks are slow; some are quick. So there is no single answer to the question about how long it will take to get a short sale approved.

Smart sellers will ask you about your experience with their

particular lienholder, so it helps to get familiar with the typical time—if there is such a thing—each lender takes to process a file.

Top agents will explain the time frame in such a way that it sets appropriate expectations and encourages quick action when needed.

With luck and persuasion, your seller will listen, especially when any inaction could have very serious consequences.

## The Biggest Complaints About Short Sales and Why They're Wrong

As important as great listening skills are to your success as a short sale specialist, there is a group of people you should not listen to—the naysayers.

You see, if I stood around the watercooler long enough, I would hear lots of complaints about short sales.

The fact is that selecting a unique niche such as short sales can really boost your income and fuel your real estate career for years to come.

In the biggest recession since the Great Depression, my staff and I have helped agents to close almost a half billion dollars in short sales.

Here are the three biggest complaints about short sales, and why they're wrong.

### Complaint No. 1: *Short sale lenders don't pay fair commissions to agents.*

*Why That's Wrong:* In 2013, the average short sale was approved by the short sale lender with a 6 percent commission to be split between listing and selling agents.

While the fact may remain that short sale listings involve slightly more work than traditional listings, the truth is that if you do your job right, you can get tons and tons of referrals from one short sale transaction. Each short sale is a gift that keeps on giving.

**Complaint No. 2:** *Short sale lenders never approve anything and always want top dollar for the property.*

*Why That's Wrong:* While it is true that the short sale lender is looking to earn as much of their lost income as possible, banks often recognize that it's a better financial decision to cut their losses now as opposed to paying the costs associated with foreclosure.

To this end, there are even financial incentive programs available in order to motivate distressed borrowers to participate in a short sale.

**Complaint No. 3:** *Short sales take too long.*

*Why That's Wrong:* A short sale can often take one to three months for approval (even longer). However, when the short sale package is submitted complete the first time, short sale time frames are shaved down to a fraction of the norm.

Into 2014 and beyond, there are many reasons to embrace the short sale transaction and other niches as good sources of business.

However, if you hang around the watercooler too long, you just may begin to believe what you hear. Make sure you are listening to the right sources of information!

## Disclosure Advice from Auntie Mabel

Everyone has an Auntie Mabel.

You know, she's that sweet yet tough little lady who everyone loves. She was the one who taught you manners. She expected you to do the right thing. Whether it was writing a thank-you note for the crisp dollar bill she gave you for your birthday or helping the less fortunate. She was the voice of conscience.

You listened to what Auntie Mabel said.

In real estate, more agents should remember their Auntie Mabel, and this is especially true when it comes to making **disclosures** of material facts.

A few years back, my office provided short sale processing and negotiation services for a local agent. This agent had the property listed as a traditional sale—whereby the lienholders would be paid in full.

Yet no buyers were interested in the property because the **list price** was too high.

So she lowered the price, and suddenly her traditional sale became a short sale. Yet she and the seller neglected to disclose to the buyer that at the current price, the transaction was now a short sale.

Several weeks later, when they figured it out, the buyer and the buyer's agent were enraged.

Although the obvious advice is to "disclose, disclose, disclose," I could not help but be curious as to how the transaction got to this point. Clearly, someone was not doing her homework.

When you take a new property listing, you must always order a preliminary title report or property profile immediately. This document will show you whether the property is overencumbered.

With the help and support of a title insurance officer, you can immediately confirm whether a clear title can be transferred. When an offer is accepted, share that report with the buyer.

So why is it that nobody knew that the property was overencumbered? Why didn't the buyer's agent look into the liens before or shortly after writing the offer? Was someone not listening to the obvious facts in this case? Why would the listing agent not fully disclose to all buyers or prospective buyers that this was a short sale?

Always listen to your Auntie Mabel . . . or your conscience.

Review title reports at the beginning of the process, and always make sure that you have made the proper disclosures—disclosures of any sort of material fact. Of course, if you are not sure whether a property is overencumbered, by all means do a little homework.

## ADVANCING TO NEW TERRAIN

### *Take Good Listening Skills to the Bank*

Have you ever felt that the person you were talking to wasn't actually listening? Maybe the other individual wasn't looking at you or maybe that person was reading text messages while you were relating some information.

It's a little bit disconcerting when this happens. If you're like me, you continue speaking in hopes that the other person is really listening to you. But often, they're not.

According to research reported in *Interplay: The Process of Interpersonal Communication*, adults spend an average of 70 percent of their time engaged in some sort of communication; of this, an average of 45 percent is spent listening.

But listening is not the same as hearing. Many of us have acute hearing skills. We can hear a high-pitched note or a whisper, but are you really listening? Are people really listening to you?

One component of success in real estate—regardless of the market—is strong listening skills. And believe it or not, our listening skills get worse as we get older.

Sadly, however, it is those very listening skills that you may need in order to get your next real estate transaction all the way to the closing table. Agents who are good listeners are more productive and close more deals because they better understand the needs of the client and what is expected of them.

### *Five Techniques to Improve Your Listening Skills*

For many people, effective listening is something that needs to be learned. With so many distractions around us, we often tend to tune out instead of tuning in.

**Technique No. 1: *Pay attention.***

Paying attention to those who are speaking is a key step to effective listening. A good listener must be prepared to pay attention. This may mean aligning the body in a certain way or making eye contact—giving the individual your undivided attention.

Paying attention also means turning off your idle thoughts—what time you need to pick up your kid from school or the e-mail you need to send to your newest buyer prospect. If you struggle with mind chatter like this, take notes while listening.

**Technique No. 2: *Demonstrate that you are listening.***

Visual cues will show the other person that you are listening. You can lean in or nod in acknowledgment. The idea is not just to listen but to encourage your client or prospect though your body language.

Concentrate on the speaker's words, gestures, and expressions. This will assist you in understanding the speaker's feelings. Look for a nod of approval of a certain backyard or style of kitchen cabinet, and you can bank that information for use when showing additional properties or closing the sale.

**Technique No. 3: *Decode what you've seen and heard.***

Absorb all that you have seen and heard and create your meaning. Ask open-ended questions to make sure that you actually interpreted the information correctly. For example, "You say that you like ranch style homes? Can you point out a few that you really like?"

When you give the client a chance to restate a thought more clearly, you will have a better picture of exactly what he or she wants.

**Technique No. 4: *Observe nonverbal cues.***

In addition to paying attention to the meaning of the words spoken, you'll also need to understand the nonverbal cues you observed. Were the gestures, the tone of voice, and the words all in agreement? Or did the words say "yes," but the body says "no"?

In a business relationship, some people feel a little bit uncomfortable about expressing their candid thoughts. That's why it's important to observe other cues. These nonverbal gestures and actions reveal inner thoughts, attitudes, and emotions that may not have been expressed verbally.

**Technique No. 5: *Paraphrase.***

It's important for effective listeners to confirm understanding. To do that, you can paraphrase or reword what you heard and observed. For example, you can say, "It sounds like you really like a kitchen with granite countertops and a double oven, preferably of stainless steel."

Politicians frequently paraphrase during interviews and public forums not only as a way to respect those in the audience that may not have heard the question but also as a way to cement the inquiry and buy time to put together their thoughts. When you paraphrase, you demonstrate that you are truly concerned about the interests of the speaker.

As a real estate professional, it is important for you to connect with clients, prospects, and affiliates. After all, you don't want them to feel as if a text message, an incoming call, or even the person down the hall is more important than they are.

When you demonstrate that you are listening, it helps to cement relationships, to learn, and, as a result, to be more efficient in whatever comes your way.

Listening also builds trust. When communication is poor, mistakes increase, and relationships breakdown. As a result, opportunities for sale are missed.

If you are seeking to strengthen business relationships, to enhance your professional image, to and improve your sales effectiveness, then all you need to do is listen.

When you listen to your clients, you show them that you only have eyes for them—and that can lead to more closed deals and lifelong referrals.

## How to "Listen" Clients into Buying

Have you ever been oversold? I have, and it generally rubs me the wrong way. In fact, when someone is trying to oversell me, I sometimes walk right out of the store and out of that salesperson's life forever.

When a salesperson oversells, he or she actually talks himself or herself out of the sale. Selling a home is not a process of convincing someone to buy.

Instead, a sale is made when you have probed so well that you learn what the prospect wants—and then recommend suitable options or solutions.

If you are new to sales, you may try to talk prospects into buying. When you are more experienced, you try to listen for openings and utilize what you've heard (or observed) to facilitate the buying process.

Top-producing real estate agents have such finesse that they can actually "listen" people into buying. This not only means that they delve deeply for needs and wants but also suggests that they pay more attention to how the prospect reacts than to what has been said.

### Watch for Verbal and Nonverbal Cues

There's a certain feeling in the air when the prospect is ready to go ahead, and there is often a distinct change in the prospect's body language and behavior when he or she is ready to buy. Look out for these potential buying cues:

- The prospect has been moving along at a smooth pace and suddenly slows down. This means that the prospect is making a final analysis or rationalizing a decision.

- The prospect speeds up. Often, prospects move more quickly when they are excited about what's to come.
- The prospect asks lots of questions. Questions about the included personal property or about the operation of a specific appliance are good signs of buyer motivation.
- The prospect inquires about general terms of purchase or the specific details of a property (such as tax rate or school district). Many buyers start asking questions about initial investment, closing date, and so on, which is a good indicator of interest.

After you have observed some of these cues, ask a few light questions to make sure you are reading your prospect correctly.

## Put Your Foot in Your Mouth

Some agents start relying so much on positive home buying cues that they rush the process. Rushing the sales process can cause you to lose sales.

Even though you may have done this a million times before, the prospective buyer has not. Each prospect should always get your full presentation in order to make sure that he or she is making a well-informed decision.

Once you are fairly certain that the buyer wants to move forward, ask a "closing the sale" question. When you ask a question from which you expect an answer confirming that the prospect wants to go ahead with the purchase, one of two things will happen:

- The prospect gives you a "yes" or an answer that indirectly confirms his or her desire to go ahead with the sale.
- The prospect raises an objection or asks for more information that will enable him or her to make a decision.

If you start talking before the prospect answers, you may lose control of the negotiations.

Let prospects be silent or converse privately. Those "awkward" silences could work to your benefit.

That's why you should always wait for folks to respond before you speak, and that's why it is so important to keep quiet after you ask your "closing the sale" question. If you have a big mouth, this would be the time to literally put your foot in it and keep yourself quiet.

Listening usually starts with questions, but it also includes nonverbal cues. When you notice the cues and ask the right questions, you will get all the information you need to close more sales—just as long as you remember to put your foot in your mouth.

## Shut Up and Sell

Almost every book on sales suggests that the salesperson needs to keep his or her mouth closed and focus primarily on listening to verbal cues from the buyer. That's what I'm advocating, too.

Real estate coach and author Bernice Ross uses the phrase "shut up and sell" in her article to address the fact that agents need to be good listeners.

Salespeople, by nature, are very gregarious. Her point, however, is that if you actually listen to your client and hear his or her wants and needs, you will be able to address the needs more quickly and efficiently than if you spend your time acting like a blabbermouth.

Here's the funny thing. While I completely understand and agree with Ross, I have an additional interpretation of the phrase "shut up and sell."

During the Great Recession, many agents faced financial and business challenges. And if you surrounded yourself with those folks, you may have noted that they were troubled and, as such, did lots and lots of complaining.

I find those who complained and those who continue to complain about the real estate market to be very exhausting.

I see these folks all the time. They are friends and colleagues; they are even people who I have done business with before.

You know them, too. They say things like "When is the market going to return to normal?" or "I closed so many deals in 2005. I wish I could close more now."

Well, I have news for these folks. Whatever the market is today—right now as you read this book—is the new normal. You need to embrace it.

It is entirely possible to close just as many transactions as you did in 2005. You may need to approach the real estate market differently.

You may need to learn and grow. You may need to change your marketing, your advertising, and some of your other strategies. But the business is here; it is what you make of it.

I think that it was Gandhi who said, "Action expresses priorities." Good, sound advice, I'd say. Through our actions, we can express our priorities.

So if you sit around the office all day and complain about the real estate market and how it needs to return to "normal," what priorities are you expressing through this action (or inaction)? What messages are you expressing through your complaints?

Instead, I'd advise an alternate method to jumpstart your career for the future: get to work, listen, and "shut up and sell."

---

Watch an informative video that contains just about everything you need to know to negotiate short sales on the *Been There, Done That* resource page at www.melissazavala.com

# KNOW WHEN TO QUIT
## The Principle of Acceptance

Let's face it; everyone fails. Expecting to breeze through everything you do without a hiccup is unrealistic and sets you up to fall harder when you actually do fail.

The truth is that when you become so focused on avoiding failure, this prevents you from gaining resiliency, a trait that is vital to your ability to overcome obstacles.

Because we are often so obsessed with success and achievement, failure can be made to feel like the worst possible thing that could ever happen. The reality is that failure is common, and so is overcoming it and pushing through to more successful endeavors in the future.

Even where a failure cannot be salvaged, there is always something to be learned from it.

The great novelist and playwright Samuel Beckett once said, "Ever tried. Ever failed. No matter. Try again. Fail again. Fail better."

Like Beckett implies, you won't believe what you can accomplish by attempting the impossible with the courage to repeatedly fail better.

Even on your very best day when you have tried your hardest or gone all the way to the top in order to overturn a decision, you may find that your real estate transaction is a "no" and not a "go."

For this reason, the ability to handle rejection is required.

You must also be able to face your clients even when you do not have good news to share.

Being involved in the distressed property world, negotiating short sales, or participating in any sort of real estate activity involves lots of ups and downs, highs and lows.

Anyone seeking success in real estate must be mentally prepared for the fact that there will be good and bad, acceptance and rejection.

Some rejections can be overcome, and others cannot. It's important to be objective and remember that the time spent wallowing in those rejections can take away your ability to close more deals, make more money, and help more people.

## *Leading a Horse to Water*

I'm sure that you're familiar with the adage "You can lead a horse to water, but you can't make him drink." But do you know what it really means?

From an equestrian standpoint, the saying is very clear. With a good halter and a rope, a well-trained horse may be led obediently. Most horses will follow a handler to the water source.

On the other hand, when arriving at the water's edge, a horse may shy away, possibly scared by the ripples or the reflection. While you may be able to get the horse to the water, you may not be able to control whether the horse will drink.

When working in real estate, the same adage applies. Of course people are not horses, but the analogy is a strong one. The final result is not always within your control.

As a buyer's or seller's agent, you can only do so many things in order to get the job done. But at the end of the day, it is not your signature that needs to be on the dotted line in order for the deal to close.

You can bring a ready, willing, and able buyer to a home, but if the seller changes his or her mind about selling, there may be little that you can do to overcome that objection.

## The Rules Are the Rules

When it comes to short sales, mortgage lenders evaluate each file with respect to specific guidelines. And there are certain kinds of transactions that follow state or federal government guidelines to the letter of the law.

There is no getting around these guidelines. I've researched it. I've seen clients spend thousands of dollars in legal fees in an attempt to circumvent these guidelines with no success.

When you're in a situation where you are up against guidelines, policies, and rules, it may be time to accept the fate of the transaction and move on.

Some lenders say that they will only permit a short sale if there is a viable hardship, and these lenders may have specific factors for determining the hardship. Others may say that they will only participate if the borrower has missed two payments.

With some of the state first-time homebuyer loans, no matter how destitute the borrower, if the borrower has violated one of the other terms of the note, the lender will not move forward no matter what. I know this; I've been down this road before.

Yet when I tell some agents that a certain transaction will likely not be successful, and they should advise the borrower to discuss alternate options with an attorney, sometimes agents still want to push and prod and cannot cut the cord.

While I understand that an agent genuinely wants to help the clients, there are certain situations where this is just not possible.

It is best to recognize these situations from the get-go, be as helpful as possible, and just move on. You are not providing value for your client when you waste time on a sale that will very likely not close.

## *Ways to Address Negative Outcomes*

Just imagine the countless hours lost on something that will never come to fruition. It's like the horse that doesn't drink—the real estate transaction; you can do everything right, but it just may not be able to close.

It's important to recognize the situations that are unworkable and move away from them as soon as possible.

Here are some ways to address and evaluate negative outcomes.

### Way No. 1: *Ask questions.*

When you are involved in a tricky transaction, ask questions, and evaluate both verbal and nonverbal cues. Try to identify from the start whether you are actually going to be able to close. If not, consider whether what you are doing is an effective use of your time.

### Way No. 2: *Seek expert advice.*

If experts advise you that what you are seeking to achieve is unlikely, move on. Consult a minimum of three experts (your broker and perhaps two other local brokers) before making a decision.

### Way No. 3: *Be honest with your client.*

Don't promise the moon if you cannot even deliver the stars. Be honest with your clients, and let them know that what they are trying to achieve may not happen and they should begin to consider alternative options.

### Way No. 4: *Don't cry over spilled milk.*

If you bottled up all the time you spent crying over your spilled milk or putting effort into deals that did not or will not close, and instead you channeled that energy and time into lead generation or other money-making opportunities, think of how much more you could grow your business.

Lamenting what could've or would've happened is not productive or healthy. Move on, and you will achieve big!

It's admirable to be passionate about what you do, and most agents that I know are so passionate that it is hard for them to let go when they see that things are not going their way.

Not only do you need to be able to face the possibility of failure, but you also need to be able to professionally face your clients with bad news and help them to move forward.

When you have trouble letting go, simply recognize that you have done your best and that there are situations that are beyond your control.

Since you cannot control the outcome, accept it, let go and move on. Seek new and different opportunities to help more people and make more money.

## ADVICE FROM THE FRONT LINE

### *How to Stop a Foreclosure*

At the beginning of the Great Recession, when banks did not yet have policies for addressing the influx of distressed borrowers, it was fairly easy to get a foreclosure date postponed.

In fact, it was often so easy that a borrower or agent could call the lender and, in a single phone conversation, request consideration for a loan modification and immediately receive postponement for a pending foreclosure auction date.

However, once the banks began to increase their Loss Mitigation Department staff and create guidelines for short sale and loan modification review, foreclosures came fast and furious.

I often receive phone calls from agents who are about to take listings on properties with looming foreclosure dates. They ask my advice and often want me to assist them in processing their short sale and obtaining a foreclosure date postponement.

Since the foreclosure date is generally just days away, my advice to those agents is that they must be quick and efficient in taking the listing and obtaining a buyer for the property.

Even then, there would be absolutely no guarantee that the seller's mortgage lender would want to entertain a short sale so late in the game. However, we could certainly give it the old college try.

Often, the agents return a few days later and send me some items for the short sale package, but frequently, those agents fail to understand that there is no guarantee that the bank will postpone the foreclosure auction date just because the property is currently available for sale.

Many agents are misinformed. Somewhere down the road, they have heard or understood that when you take a short sale listing and put it on the MLS, the bank will immediately cease all foreclosure activity.

This is false. As long as the mortgage lender is proceeding according to law, the lender can foreclose at any time. The lender is not required to halt a foreclosure auction just because they have received a pile of paperwork.

While it is hard for some sellers and agents to remember, short sale is a form of debt settlement. It is the lender who can decide whether to settle the debt or not.

## Never Wait Until the Last Minute

Distressed borrowers often wait until the very last minute in order to hire an agent to help them sell their home in a short sale. However, the best time to list a home as a short sale is not after the auction date has been scheduled and definitely not when the sheriff has pulled up in front of the house.

Spread the word: an agent experienced with distressed properties can help a borrower, but needs to be given more than a two-day window in order to do so. Give me a break. Rome wasn't built in a day.

People need time to do their jobs effectively. Sellers and agents cannot wait until the last minute, and then expect that the bank to agree to a foreclosure postponement at the eleventh hour.

When you don't plan ahead, it's often hard to avoid a negative outcome.

## When Your Short Sale Buyer Takes a Hike

Another unfortunate outcome in the short sale transaction occurs when a buyer backs out of the transaction after several weeks or months of lender negotiations.

It has probably happened to you before. In fact, it is all too common. The short sale negotiation process goes on too long, the short sale contract wasn't airtight, and the buyers disappear. They are "gone with the wind."

There are many things that a short sale listing agent can do in order to ensure a really solid short sale transaction. One such thing (and it is very, very easy) is to be a good communicator.

On all of the short sales handled by my staff, we send out a weekly status report. An e-mail such as this one can be sent to the buyer's agent, to the seller, and to any other designated party to the transaction.

This simple five-minute activity demonstrates that the short sale is still progressing, albeit often very slowly.

Another thing that can be done in order to ensure that your short sale does not evoke memories of Scarlett and Rhett is to write an airtight counteroffer.

Consider all of the items in the contract that may not be approved by the short sale lender. Before submitting the offer to the mortgage lender for approval, create a counteroffer that addresses any open-ended parts of the purchase and sale agreement.

A third way to help ensure that the buyer does not walk away in the midst of the short sale negotiations is to open escrow or put the buyer's deposit into trust.

Depending upon where you live, this may not be an option. However, there are some significant benefits to using this technique, if it is available to you.

Unless a short sale buyer has unlimited funds, requiring a deposit will aid in assuring that the buyer is not doing further shopping during the short sale process.

So the next time you are negotiating a short sale contract, try these three methods. They might actually help you to avoid failure and close the short sale transaction with the very first short sale buyer that comes your way.

## Agents, Can You Deliver?

Real estate agents often get excited at the prospect of a listing appointment—especially if they have not had one in a while. Often, agents begin using their mental calculators and spending their commission checks at the same time that the seller is signing the listing agreement.

But as you and I well know, there's a lot that goes on between the listing date and the closing date. And it is the agent's responsibility to deliver: that's what he or she is hired to do.

But can you deliver? Can you bring a ready, willing, and able buyer to the closing table? Or did you bite off more than you could chew?

While it is admirable to be a jack-of-all-trades, it is generally unlikely that a single agent can have experience selling land, commercial buildings, apartment houses, new construction, residential properties, ranches, and mobile homes among other things.

The same applies to the distressed property world. Now that short sales have been a common transaction for several years, agents and consumers alike may be under the false impression that a distressed property transaction is very easy—that everyone can list, sell, and negotiate a short sale in no time flat.

## Can Generalists Negotiate Short Sales?

While short sales have become more common, they still require certain specified knowledge. This specific knowledge includes being attuned to the subtle nuances required in order get a transaction through the bank's system quickly and efficiently.

## How to Differentiate a Generalist from a Short Sale Specialist

### Way No. 1: *Relocation assistance*

A short sale specialist will be able to immediately identify whether a seller may or may not qualify for some sort of **relocation assistance** at closing. While the specialist cannot guarantee the short sale lender's response, an agent experienced with short sales can immediately assess and identify which loans will not qualify for the incentive money.

### Way No. 2: *Lien evaluation*

A short sale specialist will immediately look into institutional and noninstitutional liens. He or she will not wait until the short sale is approved in order to research personal liens (such as tax liens or abstracts of judgment) that may impede the closing.

### Way No. 3: *Lender documentation*

A short sale specialist will know which documents need to be collected at the very beginning of the transaction—at the listing appointment. He or she will immediately identify whether you need a 4506-T, whether the lender has special documents, or whether a profit and loss statement will be required.

## Nobody Knows Everything

In Guy Kawasaki and Shawn Welch's book *APE*, Kawasaki wrote about trustworthiness. He stated, "Trustworthiness means that people can depend on you because you are honest, forthright, and effective."

He continued by saying, "Tell people what you don't know. No one knows everything. There's nothing wrong with this. You can build trust explaining what you don't know. Then people will believe you when you say you do know something."

If a real estate agent's job is to provide excellent service and to get a deal closed, then he or she needs to be trustworthy. Part of trustworthiness involves not taking a listing outside of your area of expertise.

A better solution would be to explain to your prospective clients that something is not within your area of expertise and that you would not want them to be disappointed if you could not deliver. However, you would be more than happy to refer them to an excellent specialist that can assist them.

When you admit that you are not a generalist, your prospective clients will trust you more and refer you to others. In doing so, you won't burn any bridges to future business. You would be silly to bite off more than you can chew. You might choke.

---

## ADVANCING TO NEW TERRAIN

### *When It's Time to Move On*

One of my very good friends, who was an extremely busy short sale listing agent at the height of the Great Recession, was stewing because his short sale was taking what he felt to be an inordinate amount of time.

He has closed lots of short sales, and his theory was that this particular deal shouldn't take very long to get approved because there are now fewer short sales than there were back in 2010. Since the banks are working fewer short sales, they should be moving more quickly.

My friend's theory is a good one, but the truth is that the same kinds of issues and problems that arose in 2010 continue to plague the distressed property market.

Inefficient or poorly trained employees at the lending institutions and long wait times are lingering issues that have not changed although our nation is now experiencing economic growth. With less short sales overall, fewer loss mitigation employees are required. So it stands to reason that time frames remain about the same.

## Are You Working a Deal That Will Not Close?

Oftentimes, when real estate agents do not have a lot of active prospects, they become extremely focused on the ones that they have—even if those folks are not ready, willing, or able to get to the closing table in the near future.

For example, I've seen agents show fifty or more properties to a single investor in hopes that the investor will become enamored of just one—when the truth is that the investor is looking for a specific return on investment that is unrealistic in the current market.

I've also seen agents attempt to hold together a transaction that is barely salvageable—a short sale on a $100,000 property with four mortgages, a bankruptcy, and a $6,000 homeowner's association lien.

Generally, it is the lack of leads that causes agents to grasp at deals that may never close.

Consider this: if you have ten deals in the pipeline and one deal falls through, you still have 90 percent of your business.

While sensitive to your clients' needs, you are probably not too concerned about where your next dollar is coming from. You are not worried; you have only lost 10 percent of your business.

However, if you have two deals in the pipeline, and one transaction falls through, you have lost 50 percent of your business. Your income is cut in half. You are not thriving. Instead, you are struggling to stay afloat.

The truth is that while it takes a certain expertise to work the distressed property market, a real estate professional needs to recognize that his or her chief role is that of lead generator.

A significant period of time each day needs to be devoted to lead generation if you are to continue to be successful despite any changes to the market or the economy.

## Successful Real Estate Lead Generation in Any Market

In order to more easily let go of those transactions or clients that are teetering on the brink, it's a good idea to spend a little bit of time each day on lead generation. Here are ten tips for lead generation that work in any market—not just a distressed one.

### Tip No. 1: *Network, make new friends, and keep the old.*

Attend local and regional networking events. Socialize with friends. Make a concerted effort to get face-to-face with as many new and old friends as you possibly can.

While it's generally not a good idea to over promote, when you are interacting with others, you create top-of-mind awareness—even if you are only at a block party or little league game.

### Tip No. 2: *Stay disciplined, and work your plan.*

Develop a daily, weekly, and monthly plan and stick to it. As we already discussed, it's generally not a good idea to try an activity once and then complain that it isn't generating leads.

Consistently work the same plan for days, weeks, and months. It's the follow-up and the consistency that will command attention.

### Tip No. 3: *Develop a brand.*

Make sure that your online persona, your website, and your print material all create a cohesive message about what you have to offer. First impressions matter.

Whether you meet someone on the street or they find you online, you want them to get a favorable impression of you and your real estate services.

### Tip No. 4: *Provide items of value.*

One of the most effective ways to generate a lead is by offering an item of value.

Whether it's an e-book outlining the first-time home buyer's experience or a free comparative market analysis, when you offer a free item of value, it's easy to capture a lead and a follow-up.

### Tip No. 5: *Follow up.*

Developing a consistent follow-up plan is an important part of nurturing a lead. Some leads will convert into buyers or sellers right away, and others may convert in six months or a year.

The only way to maintain top-of-mind awareness is to follow up. Not to mention that if you have spent so much time and effort on generating leads, it would be foolish to let them slip through your fingers.

### Tip No. 6: *Create a strong online presence.*

Since so many home buyers and home sellers begin their search on the Internet, that's where you want to be. It's not enough just to have a website.

You need to create a strong online presence through social media, video, and blogs.

### Tip No. 7: *Use video.*

Visitors who watch videos stay on a website an average of two minutes longer than visitors that don't. That's probably why they say, "A picture is worth a thousand words."

When you employ video in your online marketing strategies, you create traction.

### Tip No. 8: *Be a supreme multitasker.*

Are your marketing efforts limited to a direct mail newsletter monthly? You've got to do more. Develop a marketing calendar that includes both online and offline activities. Reach out to your social network and stay top of mind. Don't devote countless hours to a messy deal.

Do multiple activities each day in order to get the word out that you are the real estate professional of choice.

### Tip No. 9: *Ask for reviews, testimonials, and referrals.*

Online review sites are all the rage. That's how people decide which shoes to buy or what plumber to hire. Don't be afraid to ask current and past clients to review your services online.

You'd be surprised at the number of leads you will get from individuals that saw a complimentary review of your services online.

### Tip No. 10: *Be a local expert.*

You can't be all things to all people. It's nearly impossible to be at the top of the search engines for the search terms "Los Angeles Homes for Sale" or "New York Real Estate Agent." Statistics show that it is far easier to get on page 1 of the search engines when you focus on the smaller communities or neighborhoods within the city.

Also, individuals searching for a local specialist are generally further along in their home search and will be purchasing more quickly because they have already decided exactly where they want to live. So why not start there?

The key to success in real estate is to always work your plan. You've got to be continuously generating leads each day—no matter the market, no matter your niche.

## What Bad Service Can Teach Us About Coping with Failure

One of the secrets to success in real estate is resilience, the ability to bounce back quickly from any failure or bump in the road.

My personal resilience is constantly tested when coping with short sale processing problems. Most recently, it was also challenged when some construction workers behind my office building accidentally cut into an underground cable the size of the tree trunk.

Telephone and Internet service was obliterated in a two-city block radius. Angry executives from the affected businesses were immediately out to examine the problem, all attempting to figure out how to run their businesses without phone or Internet service.

Once it was determined that the repair would not occur in five or ten minutes, my staff and I contacted local affiliates to borrow space, and our employees were back on task in less than thirty minutes.

After our makeshift workplace was up and running, I then proceeded to investigate whether the telephone company had actually been notified that a big problem needed repair.

After calling the local customer service manager and leaving a voicemail, I dialed the toll-free emergency number mentioned in her recorded message.

Fifteen minutes elapsed before a gentleman came onto the phone. He took the information and said that a technician would be out to the site by 6:00 p.m. the following day.

When I explained to him that businesses on two city blocks were without Internet and phone service, he said that all he could do was put in a ticket and arrange for a manager to call me back within two hours.

That was that.

Two hours and seven minutes later, I received a recorded message on my mobile phone to alert me that someone would be out to address the problem within twenty-four hours, and then I could "press one to leave a message for the manager."

So much for personal service.

While the telephone company was certainly not to blame for the problem as it was not their crew who made the error, the inability of the customer service representatives to provide specialized, higher-level customer service was completely frustrating.

## Navigate Poor Service in Real Estate

Here are three things that can be learned from this crazy and chaotic experience, which can help you when coping with challenges in the field of real estate.

**Takeaway No. 1: *Prepare a backup plan.***

When negotiating with a short sale lender or trying to sort out a difficult real estate problem, it's best to have two or three plans up your sleeve—just in case the first one doesn't work. Since I was unable to get decent support from customer service, I took it up a notch, using my iPhone to tweet my concerns and also to locate a few higher-level executives that might be able to help with an innovative solution.

**Takeaway No. 2: *Adapt quickly when necessary.***

After cursing and swearing for just a few minutes, I picked up the pieces, and our employees were back at work at an off-site location within thirty minutes. Being able to adapt quickly when strange things come your way (a lost buyer, an inaccurate valuation, or a plumbing catastrophe) is often the key to success in real estate.

**Takeaway No. 3: *Never talk to the hand.***

It's futile to try to get water from a stone, so don't spend much time trying. If you need to solve a tricky problem, and the person that you are working with cannot or does not know how to support you, then you have got to move on. Don't waste your voice talking to the hand.

If I had chosen to give up, taking the responses I received as gospel, I would have been dead in the water for working that day. Many people would have been disappointed and negatively affected.

Instead, I did not assume it was over because we were without phone and Internet service. I worked my backup plan and kept going. I am pleased to report that by the following morning, all systems were restored, phones and Internet were functional again, and everyone was back in business. Good lessons sometimes come out of bad experiences.

Although the unfortunate situation could not be salvaged, something was learned from it—persistence can lead to good, creative solutions to tough problems.

## How to Provide Most Excellent Customer Service

Home buyers, home sellers, and even agents call me all the time to ask my advice on some real estate matter.

These aren't necessarily home buyers or home sellers that I am already working with, and these aren't agents from my own brokerage. These are people who've come across my name or heard that I have expertise in a specific area and they seek my advice.

I'm eager to help, and the questions are usually pretty straightforward and can be answered in just a few minutes.

If the caller is a buyer or seller, I ask whether the caller is already working with a real estate agent in his or her community. Or if the caller is an agent, I ask whether the caller has spoken with his or her broker before giving me a call.

It's funny, but in most of these situations, the caller makes some sort of nasty remark about his or her agent or even the broker. Other times, the caller says that the agent is not available or doesn't have time to return a phone call.

It is because of these disparaging remarks that I often wonder . . . if what sets a good agent apart from a not-so-good agent is merely answering the phone or making time for a client, then it shouldn't be too hard to be that special agent, that classy agent that provides amazing customer service.

## Use First-Class Service to Overcome Obstacles

It seems to me that there are several things that agents can do in order to create that awesome relationship with their clients; some of these suggestions are just as easy as answering the phone and making time to meet a client.

Here are three ways that agents can stay classy.

**Way No. 1:** *Never defer to e-mail when delivering bad news.*

Didn't get the property of their dreams? Didn't get approved for the loan? Foreclosure date was not postponed? Those are all messages that need to be delivered in person or on the telephone: not in a phone message, not over e-mail, not by an assistant, and definitely not via text.

**Way No. 2:** *Admit what you don't know.*

A huge component of a real estate agent's success is dependent upon his or her trustworthiness. This means that people can trust you because you are honest and effective. As such, you need to tell people what you know and what you don't.

Don't take a commercial listing if you don't have experience in that area, and don't promise that you can get a short sale approved if you've never negotiated one before. When you admit what you don't know, you demonstrate integrity and that leads to respect.

**Way No. 3:** *Handle rejections with poise and self-control.*

Tape your mouth shut or put your foot in it, if necessary. I once had an agent get so angry about the negotiations that he said, "Put your money where your mouth is." Instead of spitting bullets, accept the facts as hurdles on the road to success. You can go around them or you can jump over them. But don't stop, and definitely do not throw a tantrum.

When dealing with objections, when working with agents, and when working with other home buyers and sellers, you will have great success if you are resilient and can leave your drama at the door.

If you should happen to fail, all you need to do is "Try again. Fail again. Fail better."

And . . . in addition to that, you should always follow Ron Burgundy's advice and "stay classy."

---

Tips and tools relating to the information provided in this chapter can be found on the *Been There, Done That* resource page at www.melissazavala.com

# What Now?

I am not shy about saying that short sales have been a real boon for me. I caught the wave of business that came from the rise in distressed properties, and I never looked back. It's been quite a ride, and I wouldn't trade it for the world.

The perfect storm of high property prices, aggressive homeownership policies, and a global economic downturn led to a real estate opportunity that has paid off for me in many worthwhile ways. I have not only created wealth for my family and business, but I have also grown both as an agent and a person.

I've also helped thousands of homeowners handle a serious, life-changing, and emotionally distressing situation with dignity and great representation. That alone is enough to make all those late nights, hour-long hold times, and repeated requests for the same items worthwhile.

But as in all things, change happens. The real estate market is definitely changing from when I began working those short sales over a thousand transactions ago.

Does this change mean that the distressed property niche is no longer worth getting into? The short answer is "yes," but the longer answer is "it depends."

I say short sales can still be worth pursuing because millions of people remain underwater on their mortgages.

There are millions of others who are living paycheck to paycheck and are one paycheck away from being in or near default. Skilled real estate professionals will be needed to help these people navigate these tough and challenging transactions.

I say that the longer answer is "it depends" because the next wave of homeownership issues is already on the horizon.

Technology, variable economic conditions, and the changes to traditional financing models will create unique situations that few of us completely grasp yet. Plenty in the industry go so far as to declare short sales are "dead."

Shifts in the available loan options, tax breaks, and government assistance programs will also affect the marketplace and thus the real estate professional's ability to successfully make their mark in short selling. Like I said, it depends.

## Ready for a Character Reset?

Something else would help you determine your commitment to jumping into this niche too. It's about you and where you are in your career.

My biggest surprise—getting into the market—was the impact that being a short sale specialist would have on my character. I have learned and grown in ways I would never have guessed I would. Even my friends notice the difference.

My friends say I am a calmer, more patient, and more focused individual. I have a stronger determination than I've ever had, and my natural ability to see the end result while in the fray of a transaction has been sharpened into a very useful and reliable skill.

What I have noticed too is that these basic character traits, the principles that we have discussed in this book, are ones that can be honed. And unfortunately, they are the ones that are too often missing from the typical real estate agent's toolbox.

After hiring, training, and sometimes having to fire dozens of real estate professionals in my brokerage office, I have often felt frustrated.

Because of this, I am devoted to doing something about it. I intend to leverage the valuable skills I have learned in short selling and translate them into training for agents. To this end, I have started by creating a daily planner for real estate professionals.

This planner is filled with tons of tips to assist agents in building their business, staying organized, and improving their follow-up skills. It helps walk you through a step-by-step plan to not only be successful but also have solid results in all areas of your work to show for it.

If you'd rather skip the hassles of the distressed property market and focus on being a darned excellent agent, my planner would be a good starting point. Sometimes it's better to get ready before you jump into the fire, and this planner can help you prepare for what's next in your real estate career.

No matter your goals, no real estate agent is born an expert. When you take the time to set out a plan and when you take advantage of all of the wonderful resources available to you throughout the real estate industry, there is no question that, as a real estate professional, you will succeed.

# Glossary

**AUCTION:** A public sale in which goods or property are sold to the highest bidder. A *foreclosure auction* refers to the public sale of a property by the trustee after the trustee has foreclosed on the property. Also known as a trustee's sale or sheriff's sale.

**BUYER'S MARKET:** A real estate climate that favors home buyers, generally indicated by lower home prices and an increased inventory of homes for sale.

**CLOSING:** The time in a real estate transaction when the property has officially changed ownership. Sometimes referred to as closed transactions.

**COUNTEROFFER:** A document often generated by a home seller after a buyer has submitted an offer to purchase. Typically, counteroffers state that the home seller has accepted the offer subject to the terms specified in this document.

**DEBT SETTLEMENT:** Also known as credit settlement or debt negotiation, this is an approach to debt reduction in which creditor and debtor agree to a reduced balance that will be regarded as payment in full.

**DEFICIENCY JUDGMENT:** An unsecured money judgment against a borrower whose foreclosure sale did not produce sufficient funds to pay the underlying promissory note or loan in full.

**DISCLOSURES:** In real estate, this is a document or group of documents that conveys information and material facts about a given property or area and which may influence an investment decision.

**DISTRESSED BORROWER:** A borrower who is unable to fully repay his or her debt due to financial difficulties—difficulties either created by personal circumstance or the terms of the loan that he or she did not fully understand or was not able to meet when originally agreeing to the loan.

**DISTRESSED PROPERTY:** A property that is in poor physical or financial condition and a term that is commonly used to refer to properties that are worth less than the amount of the owner's mortgage loan.

**ELECTRONIC SIGNATURES:** An electronic means of indicating that a person adopts the contents of the electronic message, generally sent by means of the Internet.

**EQUATOR:** An online platform or portal used by several mortgage servicing companies to process short sale paperwork and communicate with buyers, sellers, agents, and third-party service providers.

**ESCALATE:** A verb which means "to increase." In real estate, this term is commonly used to refer to the act of contacting a supervisor in order to resolve a problem or address a concern.

**ESCROW COMPANY:** A firm that acts as a neutral third party to ensure that all conditions that the buyer, seller, and lender establish in a real estate transaction are met.

**ESTIMATED SETTLEMENT STATEMENT:** A standard form used to itemize services and fees charged to the borrower by the lender or broker when applying for a loan for the purpose of purchasing or refinancing real estate. An *estimated* form is one that is created prior to closing based on assumed costs. Also known as a HUD-1.

**FANNIE MAE:** Federal National Mortgage Association (FNMA) is government-sponsored enterprise (GSE) that was created in 1938 to expand the flow of mortgage money by creating a secondary mortgage market. Fannie Mae is a publicly traded company that operates under a congressional charter that directs Fannie Mae to channel its efforts into increasing the availability and affordability of homeownership for low-, moderate- and middle-income Americans.

**FICO SCORE:** A type of credit score that makes up a substantial portion of the credit report that lenders use to assess an applicant's credit risk and whether to extend a loan. FICO is an acronym for the Fair Isaac Corporation, the creators of the FICO score.

**FINANCIAL STATEMENT:** A document that itemizes the assets and expenses of distressed borrowers, which is generally submitted to the mortgage lender in order to review the short sale.

**FORECLOSURE:** A situation in which a homeowner is unable to make principal or interest payments on his or her mortgage, so the lender—be it a bank or other entity—can seize and sell the property as stipulated per the terms of the mortgage contract.

**FORM 4506-T:** Internal Revenue Service tax form used by taxpayers to request copies of their tax information. Taxpayers can also designate other parties to receive the information.

**FREDDIE MAC:** Federal Home Loan Mortgage Corporation (FHLMC) is a stockholder-owned, government-sponsored enterprise (GSE) chartered by Congress in 1970 to keep money flowing to mortgage lenders in support of homeownership and rental housing for middle-income Americans. The FHLMC purchases, guarantees, and securitizes mortgages to form mortgage-backed securities.

**GREAT RECESSION:** In February 2010, the Associated Press added "Great Recession" to its style guide, with the explanation that "Great Recession," when capitalized, refers specifically to the recession that began in December 2007 and became the longest and deepest since the Great Depression of the 1930s.

**HAFA:** Stands for Home Affordable Foreclosure Alternatives, which is a U.S. Treasury program that offers short sale and deed-in-lieu of foreclosure options to qualified distressed borrowers in the United States.

**HAMP:** Stands for Home Affordable Modification Program, which is a U.S. Treasury program that offers loan modification options to qualified distressed borrowers in the United States.

**HARDSHIP LETTER:** A personal letter provided to the mortgage lender that states the hardship or financial challenges of the seller and why he or she needs to sell their home in a short sale.

**HOMEOWNER'S ASSOCIATION (HOA):** A corporation formed by a real estate developer for the purpose of marketing, managing, and selling homes and lots in a residential subdivision. It grants the developer privileged voting rights in governing the association while allowing the developer to exit financial and legal responsibility of the organization, typically by transferring ownership of the association to the homeowners after selling off a predetermined number of lots.

**HUD-1:** A standard form from the Department of Housing and Urban Development that is used to itemize services and fees charged to the borrower by the lender or broker when applying for a loan for the purpose of purchasing or refinancing real estate. Also known as settlement statement.

**INCENTIVE PROGRAM:** Program offered to certain qualifying distressed borrowers that provides financial remuneration or other benefits if those borrowers agree to sell their home in a short sale.

**INVESTOR:** Any person or entity that commits capital with the expectation of financial returns. Investors utilize investments in order to grow their money and/or provide an income during retirement, such as with an annuity. With respect to distressed properties, this term refers to a specific type of buyer and also the owner of the mortgage note.

**LIEN:** The legal right of a creditor to sell the collateral property of a debtor who fails to meet the obligations of a loan contract. A lien exists, for example, when an individual takes out a mortgage loan. The lienholder is the bank that grants the loan, and the lien is released when the loan is paid in full.

**LIST PRICE:** The price at which a property is offered for sale, according to the terms of the listing agreement.

**LISTING AGREEMENT:** A document executed by the seller and the seller's real estate broker that sets out the terms for the sale of a property.

**LISTING APPOINTMENT:** The time at which a seller and a real estate professional meet in order to discuss the terms of the sale of a property and execute a listing agreement.

**LOAN MODIFICATION:** Permanently restructuring the terms of the loan that may include lowering the total repayment amount required by the borrower or extending the length of time given to repay the full loan amount.

**LOSS MITIGATION:** Term used to describe a third party helping a homeowner, a division within a bank that mitigates the loss of the bank, or a firm that handles the process of negotiation between a homeowner and the homeowner's lender.

**MLS:** Stands for "multiple listing service," which is a database that shares comprehensive home information among real estate professionals.

**MORATORIUM:** A noun that means "temporary prohibition of activity." In real estate, this term refers to the ceasing of foreclosure or mortgage collection activity.

**MORTGAGE DEBT RELIEF:** Commonly referred to as tax relief, this term refers to the Internal Revenue Service Mortgage Forgiveness Debt Relief Act of 2007, a tax act that provided certain borrowers with tax relief in situations of short sale, foreclosure, or deed-in-lieu of foreclosure.

**MORTGAGE LENDER:** The lender providing funds for a mortgage or the lender that receives and manages the monthly mortgage payments.

**MORTGAGE SERVICER:** A company to which some borrowers pay their mortgage payments and which performs other services in connection with mortgages and mortgage-backed securities. The mortgage servicer may be the entity that originated the mortgage, or it may have purchased the mortgage servicing rights from the original mortgage lender. Also commonly referred to as servicer.

**POCKET LISTING:** Denotes a property where a broker holds a signed listing agreement with the seller, but where it is never advertised nor entered into the MLS or where advertising is limited for an agreed-upon period of time.

**PRELIMINARY TITLE REPORT:** The results of a title search by a title company prior to issuing a title binder or commitment to insure clear title on a given property.

**PURCHASE CONTRACT:** An agreement between a buyer and seller of real property, setting forth the price and terms of the sale. Also known as a sales contract or a purchase and sale agreement.

**REALTOR®:** A federally registered membership mark that indicates a real estate agent or real estate professional who is a member of the National Association of REALTORS® (NAR). According to NAR, the preferred usage is REALTOR® in all capital letters with the federal registration symbol. If the registration symbol is not possible, NAR prefers members to use all capital letters to indicate membership. For aesthetic purposes, the editor of this book has opted to modify the recommended format.

**RELOCATION ASSISTANCE:** Financial remuneration offered to certain qualifying borrowers who agree to sell their home in a short sale.

**RESPA:** Stands for Real Estate Settlement Procedures Act, which is a consumer protection statute that prohibits kickbacks between lenders and third-party settlement service agents in the real estate settlement process.

**SELLER'S MARKET:** A real estate climate that favors home sellers, generally indicated by higher property values and a decreased inventory of homes for sale.

**SHORT SALE:** The sale of a home for less than the unpaid balance on the loan and where the lender forgives the remaining amount due on the mortgage.

**SHORT SALE APPROVAL LETTER:** The letter generated by the borrower's mortgage lender that agrees to specific terms and conditions and approves the sale of the subject property for less than the amount owed.

**SHORT SALE LENDER:** Any mortgage lender or mortgage servicer that reviews the borrower's short sale package.

**SHORT SALE LISTING:** Any listing agreement between a seller and a real estate broker whereby the amount owed on the mortgage is more than the value of the property and where the seller's mortgage lender will need to review and ratify the sale.

**SHORT SALE NEGOTIATOR:** Any individual that aids in the processing of short sale documentation and facilitates short sale approval—either as an agent of the seller or an agent or employee of the mortgage lender.

**SHORT SALE PACKAGE:** Any group of items required by the mortgage lender in order to review and approve a short sale.

**STATEMENT OF INFORMATION:** Also called a statement of identity, this is a brief statement of facts relied on by title insurers to assist in the proper identification of persons.

**THIRD-PARTY AUTHORIZATION:** Authorization given by the mortgage holder to third parties to contact the lender in order to discuss the particulars of the designated loan.

**TITLE COMPANY:** The company that issues title insurance for the subject property.

**TITLE INSURANCE:** A form of indemnity insurance that insures against financial loss from defects in title to real property and from the invalidity or unenforceability of mortgage liens.

**TITLE REPORT:** The written analysis of the status of title to real property, including a property description, names of titleholders and how the title is held, tax rate, encumbrances, and real property taxes due.

**TRUSTEE'S SALE:** A public sale in which goods or property are sold to the highest bidder. A *foreclosure auction* refers to the public sale of a property by the trustee after the trustee has foreclosed on the property. Also known as auction or sheriff's sale.

**UNDERWATER BORROWER:** A mortgagor who owes more on the home loan than the property is worth.

*Special thanks to my family and friends for their undying support throughout this wild short sale journey: to my staff at Short Sale Expeditor® and the agents of Broadpoint Properties for their amazing dedication, to our wonderfully loyal clients who have allowed me to take them on this roller coaster, to loss mitigation employees everywhere for giving me motivation and determination, to Vickie Flaugher of Smartwoman Publishing for her hard work and entrepreneurial inspiration, to Melissa Marquardt for her abiding friendship and spectacular eye for design, and to Javier for his infinite patience even though he has listened to every one of my stories at least five hundred times. Thank you.*